To: Wayne Martin

Enjoy

All Enemies, Foreign and Domestic

A Briefing for American Citizens About the War on Terror

Kit Cessna

Bloomington, IN Milton Keynes, UK
authorHOUSE®

AuthorHouse™
1663 Liberty Drive, Suite 200
Bloomington, IN 47403
www.authorhouse.com
Phone: 1-800-839-8640

AuthorHouse™ UK Ltd.
500 Avebury Boulevard
Central Milton Keynes, MK9 2BE
www.authorhouse.co.uk
Phone: 08001974150

First published by AuthorHouse 1/25/2007

ISBN: 978-1-4259-9511-9 (e)
ISBN: 978-1-4259-8902-6 (sc)

Library of Congress Control Number: 2006911248

Printed in the United States of America
Bloomington, Indiana

This book is printed on acid-free paper.

Acknowledgements

Writing your second book is a completely different experience from writing your first one. The mystery is gone, and you attack the keyboard knowing that book writing can be done successfully. The work and difficulty are still there, however, and no book can be completed without the help of those around you. Therefore, I give my thanks to:

My beautiful and loving wife Stephanie for her presence and help along the way. Once again she stuck by me with encouragement and advice, and this work was the result.

The United States Army, 1st Special Forces, Operational Detachment-Delta (Delta Force,) of which I was a proud member for several years. For most Americans, the War on Terror began on September 11, 2001. For the soldiers of this organization, it began a long time before that and will continue far into the future. Being a member of that proud and dedicated unit, gave me the background to write this book.

Dedications

This book is dedicated to the following brave individuals:

The police officers and firefighters who lost their lives on the morning of September 11th in 2001. Amid the fire and smoke of collapsing buildings, they unhesitatingly rushed to the aid of others. These brave souls gave what President Abraham Lincoln called "the last full measure of devotion." As Americans, we should be awed and inspired by the courage that they displayed on that terrible day.

Staff Sergeant Nate Chapman of the United States Army, 1st Special Forces Group and Johnny "Mike" Span of the United States Central Intelligence Agency. Killed in action in Afghanistan, they were the first known ground casualties in this war. They were the "men in the arena," and their honored place will never be with those cold, timid souls who already want to run away.

Table of Contents

Introduction

"We learned about an enemy that is sophisticated, patient, disciplined, and lethal. It makes no distinction between military and civilian targets. Collateral damage is not in its lexicon."

9/11 Commission Report

Congress of the United States of America

Ladies and gentlemen, we live in a world that is governed by the use of deadly force. We can wish that this was not so but, that wish will not change the facts. The history of mankind has been a history of conflict and the future of mankind will be no different. Civilizations have come and gone; others will follow, and all have suffered conflicts of one type or another. It appears that some factor in the very core of our nature dictates that we will be continually be at odds with one other.

Our disagreements come about for many different reasons. Sometimes our arguments are of a political nature and the conflict concerns the way a given society is structured and governed. The world has seen its share of these types of struggles, and it will see more. Other times, the fight is economic in nature and centers on the subjects of wealth and property. The locations of national boundaries are also fought over and this process will continue. Sometimes the altercation is over the subject of religion or a particular outlook on life. Sometimes, the confrontation is about a combination of all the above-mentioned subjects.

In the early twenty-first century, the United States finds itself in just such a conflict. While this fight is primarily religious in nature, there are many factors at play. National borders, military presence, and economic conditions, all play a major role, but things go much deeper than that. This war, my friends, is about the very idea of individual freedom and the future direction of human civilization. On one side you have a dedication to liberty and progression for the whole human race. On the other side you have a malignant tyranny, cloaked in ancient religious garb, which is dedicated to returning humanity to the Middle Ages. More simply put, it is the mindset of the twenty-first century west against the sixth century east.

This war did not begin with the attacks of September 11, 2001, and will not end with any particular event in Iraq or Afghanistan, or with an election in the United States. The situation that we are facing today started over ten centuries ago and has been building ever since. It will continue even when the present circumstances no longer exist. It is nowhere close to being over, and we are still in the opening phases of the fight. If you are of middle age today, your grandchildren will probably be involved in this confrontation when they are adults. For the first time since the Second World War, we face a foe who is fully capable of defeating us. The enemy can win this war and, if we continue on our present course, he just might.

You will not see landing craft full of Al Qaeda operatives coming ashore on American beaches. Battalions of radical Muslim fanatics will not descend by parachute onto your lawn. They don't possess the military power or mind-set necessary for such a direct attack, and it is not likely that they ever will. They don't have these capabilities and they don't really need them. They don't need them because what they do possess is patience, discipline, and a total focus on this conflict. With these tools, they have the ability to strike such an extreme blow to our economy and social structure that it would cease to exist as we know it. They seek to do this through the use of terror and have been carrying out attacks for decades against our nation and its interests. They will continue their attacks as long as we exist and hold influence in the world. As long as we are here, this fight will continue.

As I stated in my first book, when you are in a fight for your life, you can either be the winner or the loser. Being the winner is the recommended choice. If we are going to win this war, we will have to decide that we want to be the winners and do some things differently. Every American needs to get used to the idea that life as we knew it before 9/11 is gone, forever. As a nation, we will have to wake up and grow up. We are going to have to realize the true nature of the fight and what is at stake. Nowhere will this transformation be more important than in the attitude and mindset of the average citizen. This is the single, most critical factor in this struggle and I will tell you plainly: The current attitude and mindset of the average American citizen is the biggest potential threat that we face in this conflict. If we lose this war it will not be because of anything that our enemy was able to do, it will be because of what we have done or failed to do.

Within these pages, I will reveal the true nature of our enemies and why we must defeat them. I will explain their history and motivations, and why they do what they do. I will point out their strengths as well as their weaknesses and believe me, they have weaknesses. Most importantly, I will discuss your role and duties in protecting this nation from them. All of this I will do in plain layman's language.

There are two sides to any conflict and anyone standing on the sidelines will find it easy to criticize and point out the faults of either one. As a nation, the United States of America has made mistakes and miscalculations in dealing with other peoples, both past and present. We cannot change that and it is not my intention to try. On the other hand, nothing that we have done justifies the actions of our enemies. Analyzing past mistakes is not something that can replace loyalty and loyalty is the cornerstone of any society. History shows us that sometimes those loyalties will be tested and if that test is failed by enough people then our society is in trouble. Our loyalties are being tested now and many of our citizens are failing that test. True colors are waving in the breeze all across this land. From a hostile media that seeks to undermine all of our efforts in this war, to Hollywood celebrities who want to run away or make excuses for the foe, the domestic enemies of this nation boldly show themselves. Under our constitution they have that right, and I would not stand by and see that right taken from them. However, I also have that right and if they can speak, so can I. If they can make movies presenting their opinion of this conflict, then I can write a book doing the same thing. If they can set out each day to find ways to undermine this nation and its interests, then I am free to point out their activities and label them correctly as the actions of a domestic enemy.

I have chosen my side in this issue and I will stay on that side no matter what happens. I am one hundred percent on the side of the United States of America and I will not deviate from that anywhere in this book. Although I have gained much insight into the nature of our enemies, the primary knowledge that I seek is that which is necessary to defeat them, and it is their total defeat that I desire. I want them to be destroyed and decimated to the point where they can no longer offer a credible threat to us. In a singular fashion, I have studied this enemy for years and I know what goes on inside of his head. I understand his view of mankind and human civilization. I hold his view in complete contempt and my words will reflect that stance. You will find no political correctness here.

Thank you for reading and enjoy the book.

Kit Cessna

Baton Rouge 2007

Chapter 1

The Conflict

"History is littered with the wars which everybody knew would never happen."

Enoch Powell,

British politician

Fellow citizens, when you woke up this morning and went about your business, you did so as the citizen of a nation at war. This is not some far off regional conflict, where the outcome will have little effect on your daily life; this is a struggle for your very existence. This idea may be a bit hard for you to grasp because as wars go, this is a quiet one. There were probably no car bombs exploding in your neighborhood as you went to work and automatic weapons fire did not rattle the windows of your children's school bus. Suicide bombers did not pay a visit to your local police station, and when you voted in the last election (if you voted in the last election), you did so without being wounded or killed. All the same, you stand in the middle of a battlefield. As you conduct your daily activities a vicious enemy plots your death and the death of your loved ones. If that enemy can bring one of those plots to operational status, you and your family will probably not survive the event. There are individuals and organizations out there that view you and yours with hatred and contempt. That which you value, they see as worthless. That which you love, they hate and despise. They hate you for many reasons, but primarily because you are here with them on this planet. It is not a matter of the property that you own or the money that you make. Rather, it is your very existence that offends them. It has always offended them and it always will. They don't like you and, if they can, they are going to get rid of you. These

1

people have already murdered thousands of your fellow citizens in this conflict and they will kill thousands more before it is over.

This war did not start yesterday and it will not be over tomorrow. The date of 9/11 did not mark the beginning and events in Iraq, Afghanistan, or Lebanon will not signal the end. This struggle began a long time ago and it will go on long past our lifetimes. In one way or another, this fight is occurring on every part of globe and the whole planet is a battlefield. Every nation and culture is currently caught up in the struggle or eventually will be. The reasons for the conflict have varied as the centuries have passed, but the essence of the fight is the same. It is good against evil and what remains to be seen is which of those will prevail in the end. This is not a contest between cultural perfection and lack of perfection. A situation such as that does not exist. Nor is it a contest between a society that has made no mistakes and one that has made many; neither does that situation exist. No, this is simply a contest between those individuals and societies that are beneficial to mankind and those that are not. It is a matter of overall good versus overall evil, and it is important to identify who is who.

The Good Guys

"I always consider the settlement of America with reverence and wonder, as the opening of a grand scene and design in providence for the illumination of the ignorant and the emancipation of the slavish part of mankind all over the earth."

John Adams

Second President of the United States

There are two sides to any conflict: there is the "us" and there is the "them." The "us" is the United States of America and the bulk of the western world, known as "Western culture." It can be said that the United States is the present leader and guardian of that culture. The "them" is all of those who are opposed to the values and ideals of our culture. It really is no more complicated than that. Since its

2

inception, western culture and civilization has been the best hope for the future of the human race. It is light opposing darkness and kindness standing against cruelty. At its core, western ideology is centered on the right of human beings to live in peace and happiness. The fundamental conviction of this culture is that the natural state of mankind is one of freedom and prosperity and that a practicing civilization should work toward those ends. Many civilizations of the past kept the light of this belief alive. Ancient Greece was one the main birthplaces of this divine idea and the human race owes that nation an eternal debt of gratitude. The Roman Republic was probably a more functional model of this thought process while it lasted. However, with Rome's slow transition into an empire, many of these ideals were abandoned in the pursuit of global power, setting the stage for eventual collapse. After the fall of Rome, mankind endured centuries of brutality under warring dictatorships while brave individuals struggled to keep the precious idea alive. With the coming of the Renaissance, western culture re-arose and again, light began to replace darkness. All of the nations and cultures that played a part in the survival of this ideology should be commended for it. There is one nation however, that has taken it further than all others.

The United States of America is God's gift to the human race. There has never been a nation such as ours and, if we go away, there will probably never be another. We have done more good for mankind that any other civilization. Because of the sacrifices that we have been willing to make, hundreds of millions of human beings now live in the warm light of freedom. Around the globe countless people no longer live in fear because we removed some murderous thug from power. Because of our leadership and technological prowess, this planet is capable of supporting life on a scale never seen before, and the overall standard of living is rising all around the planet. The magnitude of our economy provides a stable platform for the development of other nations and cultures.

Our generosity with our wealth is unprecedented in human history, and the amount that we have contributed to others cannot be counted. When there is a natural disaster, we are the first ones to step up and help, and there have been times that we have sent help to others even while we were suffering from disasters of our own. Cruel individuals and regimes have fallen to our economic and military prowess, and the light of freedom is slowly spreading in places that only knew darkness. All across the planet individuals and societies are beginning to realize that freedom is actually possible and lies within their grasp. Since our inception, we have been a nation of compassion and caring and have continually sought to better the world.

One of the most compelling examples of our essential goodness as a nation and culture has been represented in our actions after 9/11. Rather than going to Afghanistan to simply seek vengeance, (which was well within our power to do,) we set about improving life for the citizens of that unfortunate land. No other nation would have done anything but the former. After the fall of Saddam Hussein, we again set about making a better life for the Iraqi people. The United States has spent billions of dollars and thousands of lives so that the citizens of this far away land could have a chance to experience some of the same blessings that we enjoy. History shows us that no other nation could or would make such a commitment. The fact that we are even willing to try sets us apart.

Are we a perfect society or culture? No, we are far from that. We have made plenty of mistakes and we will continue to make them. We have treated others with brutality and contempt upon occasion and there are some dark spots on our past. We have misjudged people and situations and sometimes proceeded along a course without all the facts and with disregard for those affected by our actions. All of the weaknesses inherent to human beings have been displayed by us and will continue to be. There will always be those who are hurt by our actions. On the other hand, those who have benefited by our existence vastly outnumber those who have been harmed by it. When all is added up and things are measured, we are clearly the good guys. That is why the bad guys hate us so much.

The Bad Guys

"It is necessary only for the good man to do nothing for evil to triumph."

Edmund Burke

British Statesman and Philosopher

If you are going to understand this conflict, you are going to have to understand the true nature of the world around you and the simple concept of good vs. evil. We did not start this war and we do not want it in our lives. Unfortunately, reality dictates that this situation is in our lives and will be for some time to come. There is nothing that you or I can do about this fact other than to accept it and act accordingly. The history of life on Planet Earth is a history of the struggle between good and evil; and nothing has changed in modern times. Evil exists, and there really is not much that you can do about it. As long as there are human beings on this planet, some of them will be good and some of them will be bad. Many people will live their lives posing little to no consequence to those around them and will be quickly forgotten after passing. Other people will seek to do good deeds, in one way or another, and while their success will vary, they are generally remembered in a good light. Sometimes the actual results of their endeavors don't turn out well, but their overall intention was to better the world around them. Other human beings come into this world with a different set of goals. These folks come here with the idea of doing as much harm as possible. They come here for the purpose of doing evil and most of them are successful in the pursuit of that goal. Some of them take that success to great lengths; the misery that they bring lasts for generations.

Belief in the existence of total evil requires belief in the existence of the totally evil human being. I know that some of you will take issue with that belief and will attempt to enlighten me on the subject. You will point out to me that many human beings are merely a product of their environment and that not all bad people set out to become that way. In some cases, you are right. In all societies, both

5

past and present, there have been and are now individuals who have done great wrongs, and it can be said that this was not their original intent. Some of them are misguided and suffering from the lack of a proper upbringing, and some of them are truly victims of their surroundings. That being said, I still maintain that there are among us individuals who were predisposed toward evil from the moment that they drew their first breath. Every bit of their psychological makeup leans in this direction. They could no more change their ways than a dog could turn into a cat. They do the things that they do because that is who and what they are. When they bring fear and misery to others, they do so because they enjoy the task and want to do it as much as possible. No amount of rehabilitation or therapy will change their outlook on the world around them and negotiation with any such individual, or any attempt to make them see things differently, is a waste of time and effort. They are here among us today and they will be with us tomorrow. Nothing that you or I do will change this basic fact of life.

I have often speculated that these people may actually be a separate species of human being. I will not attempt to defend this position with any empirical evidence, as I have none to offer other than a lifetime spent observing them. Certainly they are like you and me when it comes to physical attributes; they have two arms, two legs, and one head, and they cannot be distinguished by visual means. On the other hand, I believe that were it possible to do an in-depth examination of their mental structure, and were it possible to lay that structure out for close examination, there would be identifiable differences. If this view could be brought to a visual manifestation, then I think that the differences would be glaring. In reality, I have presented this view point to several working homicide investigators and none of them have disagreed with me. In fact, most of them claim to have actually met these individuals. For lack of a better term, I will refer to them singularly as "the enemy" and this is who he is.

The Enemy

"If all evil were prevented, much good would be absent from the universe."

Saint Thomas Aquinas

Catholic Theologian and Philosopher

Over the centuries, the enemy has worn many different faces and has attired himself in different garb. He has sat on a throne and brutalized his own people unchecked for generations. He has launched wars of conquest and left miles of corpses behind him. He has waited in the darkness as a lone assassin, and though he only killed a few, he caused terror in many. He has commanded death camps and stood on the piles of bodies that were his victims. He has hidden himself in the veils of an ancient religion and spread fear and death around the globe. He changes his appearance and language through the years but, if you pay attention and look closely, you will see his face all around you.

You can recognize him in the demented countenance of the religious fanatic as he recruits children to become human bombs. You can see him in the smirk of the murderous dictator as he stands before an insane crowd firing a pistol into the air. He is visible in the sullen face of the convicted murderer as his sentence is passed and he waits for the day of execution. You can view him in the bitter stare of the corrupt politician who has betrayed all that he was sworn to uphold. Some have fought him and lost and generations of horror were the result of that defeat. Some have fought him and won and, in the aftermath of that victory, he would disappear for a while. There would then be a short time of peace and prosperity, but he has always come back and he always will. Millions have died or lived in misery on his account and millions will do so in the future.

Friends, I don't know why, but I have always been personally aware of him. Even as a small child, I recognized his existence although I rarely recognized his face. Now, many years past childhood, I see him easily and I see him every day in one form or another. When I was younger, I was afraid of him. I knew he was

7

there and felt fear at the thought of confronting him. That is what I felt then; now I feel differently. I have confronted him and have lived to tell about it, and in doing so, I have seen a side of him that most people never will; I have seen him afraid and I have seen him defeated. While I will never be so foolish as to turn my back on him, I will never fear him again.

I have seen his bullet-riddled corpse lying in a pool of blood and shattered concrete in the aftermath of a failed ambush. I have seen him face down in the street, victim of a murderous thug just like him. I have watched him fall to his knees in a darkened alley and beg for his life, surrounded by the soldiers that had spent days chasing him. I have seen him dragged out of a tear-gas-filled house by a SWAT Team, pleading not to be harmed, after he spent hours holding a five-year-old boy hostage. I have seen him cry like a small child in a courtroom when he realized that justice had finally turned its face on him and this time there would be no escape.

I have learned much about the enemy over the years and I come to understand why he does what he does. I know what he hates and what he seeks to destroy. He hates most everything around him, but most of all he hates those around him. He hates the fact of human life on this planet. He hates to see anyone free to enjoy their existence and the fruits of their labors. He hates love and laughter and, above all, he hates the concepts of courage and hope. He hates the thought of human beings living their lives free of fear and brutality. I know all about his hate and how deeply it is felt and I know that he will never feel any different toward the rest of us. I know other things about him as well.

I know that at the core of his being he is a coward. He seeks to spread fear because it is fear that rules him and his fears are many. In some cases, he is physically afraid of retribution for his terrible acts and knows that this may well be his fate. If he is in a position of power, he fears losing that position and will commit any act to maintain it. He lives in a world of fear and contempt, and will always view the world around him in the same manner. I don't know why the enemy is among us; I just know that he is. I suppose that he serves a purpose or he would not be here. In the end, I don't guess that the "why" matters all that much. He is here and will always be here; there is not much that we can do to change that. We have to accept his presence on this planet and do all that we can to stop him. In a nutshell, that is what this war is all about. Either good will prevail or it will be evil, and the jury has always been out. Throughout the centuries, this struggle has taken on many forms and faces, and the issues change as the years go by. The surface causes of the conflict will transform over the course of your lifetime, so it is not a good idea to become fixated on a single set of circumstances. It is better to adopt an attitude of understanding the modern version of the struggle while keeping in mind the overall picture.

Chapter 2

The Modern Version

"The enemies of freedom do not argue, they shout and they shoot."

William Ralph Inge

British clergyman and writer

Terrorism is nothing new on the planet and this present situation is not all that unique in many respects. Individuals and organizations have always sought to rule others by fear. This situation can be traced back to biblical times, and at no point in human history have we been completely free of this threat. Terrorism has been employed by governments and by those opposed to governments. It is not just the tool of the small, shadowy groups of disaffected individuals because governments have been known to use it and use it well. In fact, it can be argued that governments are actually the more efficient users of terror. An examination of the last seventy some years bear this out. During this time we have had to contend with Joseph Stalin of the Soviet Union, Adolph Hitler of Nazi Germany, Mau Tse Tung of Communist China, Pol Pot of Cambodia, and Saddam Hussein of Iraq, just to name a few. When compared to the four-thousand some years of recorded human history, seventy years represents the blink of an eye, and look at the monsters this short time period produced.

We are not that far past an era when this nation was involved in a struggle similar to the current one. The forty year face-off with international communism was about some of the same issues as our present conflict and even mirrored some of the same events. During the height of Soviet power, the world was plagued by a series of terrorist attacks carried out by groups controlled by the socialist state. Seeking to export its ideology on a global scale; Moscow funded and trained terrorist groups scurried around the planet killing and blowing things up. There were hijackings, kidnappings, assassinations and bombings galore just as there are today. There were no large scale direct attacks on U.S. soil, but that was more than likely due to the stand-off nature of the situation, rather than a lack of desire on their part to do it. Terrorism has always been here, and always will be.

The terrorist threat that we face today is different than that which we endured as a result of international communism and its desire for global domination. It is just as dangerous to our way of life, however, if not more so. If the United States government and the national news media do not have the courage and honesty to tell you the simple truth, then I will. The situation that we face today comes from religious radicals acting for religious purposes and these enemies are from the Middle East and the Persian Gulf. Ladies and gentlemen, fools believe that this war is not about religion. Fools believe that it can be explained in other ways, and fools get on my television set and spout that garbage at me almost every day. Steeped as we are in destructive political correctness, it seems that we are determined to blind ourselves to this simple fact. Our enemies shout it in our face, but we don't appear able to hear their message. When an Iranian author is subjected to a global death threat and the threat is approved by high ranking Muslim holy men, it's about religion. When a series of cartoons featuring the prophet Mohammed are published in a Danish newspaper and the publication results in riots all over the Islamic world, this is a clear indication that the struggle is over religion. When an inconsequential filmmaker in Holland is murdered for making some low level criticisms of Islam in one of his seldom watched films; guess what, it's about religion. When second generation Canadians plot to behead their Prime Minister in the name of Islam, it's about religion. When native born Americans are rounded up in a Miami warehouse for plotting to blow up a building in Chicago for the same reasons, it's about religion. The politically correct crew can deny this as much as it wants and that changes nothing. Bottom line: it's about religion.

11

Over the last few years there have been times when I almost felt sorry for the enemy. I feel his frustration because it reflects my own. He has been telling us for centuries that this is about religion, but we don't seem to be inclined to believe it. He has been telling us that he hates us and our ideas and how he will destroy us sooner or later. He has told us this again and again and we seem content to ignore the message. It must be exasperating for him to have us continually discount the facts that he screams at us. Folks, this is a religious war and that reality should always stay in your thoughts. Other issues are part of the conflict, and religion does not cover the whole subject, but it is one of the main issues and don't let some idiot of a politician or newscaster tell you differently.

The history, culture, and religion of the Middle East and the Persian Gulf represent a subject that I have dedicated much time to understanding. I read about this area and what happens there, before I was a teenager. At age eleven or less, I could have recounted to you the basic history of the situation and the main players in it. Obviously, there are experts out there who possess far more knowledge on this subject than me. On the other hand, I am confident that when it comes to the average American citizen, my knowledge outweighs theirs by a considerable amount. I have studied these folks and their world since I was a child, and I have lost count of the number of books that I have read about them and their outlook on life. I have traveled to most of their nations and interacted with them daily during those trips. I have had class after class of them in front of me on federal training programs. As the years have gone by, I have taken every opportunity to get to know them and have never passed up a chance to crawl inside their heads and see what was going on. Official expert or not, I have gathered quite a lot of information on them and I will tell you again; fools believe that this war is not about religion. Our enemies believe that it is about religion, and they don't believe anything else. This thing goes back over a thousand years to the time of the Crusades and our enemies remember that time as if it were last week. The radicals in the world of Islam think of little else except this conflict and its religious undertones. If you attempt to ignore the fact that this is a religious war, you are sabotaging your ability to understand it.

The Religion of Islam

"So much wrong could religion introduce"

Titus Lucretius

1st century Roman poet

For the radicals among the Muslim cultures, religion is the single primary motivator of their existence. Unlike western Judeo/Christian culture where religion is part of life, in this part of Islam, religion is life. It is what makes them get out of bed each morning and its influence governs their every activity. Everything that they do during their day has some connection to their faith and even if they are not personally devout practitioners, they are under its influence every minute that they are awake. That is a major difference in outlook between us and them. With that simple fact; the seeds of incompatibility are already planted. Make no mistake; a situation of incompatibility is exactly what we have today.

Prior to the 11th of September 2001, you would have been hard pressed to find an American citizen that possessed any real knowledge about Islam. I suppose that can be understood, but what is not so understandable is that you would be just as hard pressed to find one today. Other than what they may glean from the ten second sound bites produced by the media, the average American knows almost nothing about the Islamic faith or the people that it controls. Much of what they do know is wrong and, unfortunately, most people are not interested in correcting the situation. Even if more Americans were so inclined, they would have limited options to sort through. Anyone looking for information of real substance from our modern press is looking at a blank wall. Not only is our current media incapable of bringing forth information with any real depth or lack of slant, they are not inclined to do so. This is a bad state of affairs and the situation will not improve until we begin to demand news from these entities instead of entertainment. In light of their failures to provide any real education, I will attempt to fill the gap.

The religion of Islam came about in the 600's and sprung up in what is now modern Saudi Arabia. Over the next few centuries, it continued to evolve and has developed into one of the world's three main religions. In modern times its influence is still increasing and it has been labeled as the fastest growing faith on earth. The reasons for this growth are many and a complete examination of this religion and its history is well beyond the scope of this work. I have studied it extensively, however, and I will leave you with some recommended titles for further reading on the subject at the end of the book. One of the main answers that I have searched for in my readings is what makes this ancient faith so appealing in modern day? Why are millions around the globe drawn to its teachings and rather restrictive way of life? What does Islam hold that the others lack and why does Islam recruit while other faiths steadily lose membership? I ask this question at every opportunity, and the answers are mixed.

The person who has been reared in this religion will simply tell you that it is the one true faith and that is the end of the matter. Actually, one has to be careful when asking this question because some of them will take the inquiry as a criticism of Islam. Yet, asking Muslims who are somewhat westernized and therefore not so sensitive, usually does not result in information that is any more revealing. Most of these individuals, while not necessarily hostile, seem puzzled by the question and have no real answer. To be fair, I don't know if you would do any better if you were to direct the same line of inquiry to devout Christians or Jews. On the other hand, understanding the appeal of this religion is part of the key to understanding the enemy in this conflict.

One of the insights that I do have in this matter came from an Indian gentleman that I had the pleasure to meet a few years ago. He was a high ranking officer in the Indian Army and had seen a lot of combat against Muslim fanatics in the Kashmir Valley and other places. At the time that we discussed this issue, he was in the United States attending an anti-terrorist tactical course in which I was an instructor. When he completed the course, he would be returning to his homeland to take command of their premier military counter terrorist unit. We found that we shared similar views on many issues, and as a result, had many long discussions on some of the subjects covered in this book. He was well educated and well spoken and when I put the question of the appeal of Islam to him, he did not hesitate to answer, indicating that it was a subject to which he had also given much thought.

Islam, he maintained, is a very dogmatic religion, perhaps the most dogmatic of them all. Judaism and Christianity leave many subjects to the will of the individual, but not the religion of Mohammed. This faith tends to give authoritarian instructions for just about every aspect of life. In Islam, there are directions for almost everything that human beings will have to contend with during their existence. That set of circumstances appeals to many people because it offers a type of implied guarantee in life. Telling someone what to do day in and day out relieves the individual of much responsibility and many people on this planet are looking to avoid as much of that burden as they can. Islam claims to have all of the answers and is perfectly willing to tell you what to do with your time. That type of thought process tends to draw people who are not inclined to look any further. In a nutshell, that was his take on the matter and, given his life experiences, I was not inclined to argue. I have heard from other people who have come from that part of the world and they tend to agree with his view on the matter. Islam offers a rigid structure for existence that provides a type of authoritarian reassurance.

For myself, I think that this explanation has some merit to it and goes a long way toward explaining the appeal of Islam. I also think that there is a bit more to it than a set of instructions. In my studies and travels, I have observed that most Islamic cultures have a much stronger sense of family and community than do most western ones. Among individuals of this faith, there is usually an automatic situation of acceptance and welcome. This is true even if the folks in question come from different nations or tribes. The family of Islam seems to transcend all other social factors and there is an understandable appeal to this set of circumstances. I think that many individuals who are introduced to Islam are attracted to it because it seems to fill some real or imagined void in their life. Other people are brought up from childhood in this faith and their devotion is understandable. There can be a sense of anonymity and isolation in much of western culture and, unfortunately, our religions do not seem to fill this gap as well for us as theirs does for them. If it sounds like I am championing their religion, believe me, I am not. I have seen the reality of life under Islam first hand, and you will not find me lining up to be converted.

It must be recognized that there is a desire within most human beings to achieve a more spiritual and meaningful existence. When this is coupled with the natural yearning to be accepted by those around them, then the result can be that normal people find themselves ensnared by religious cults, much to their eventual regret. That was the situation with the Japanese Aum Shiraniko organization and their nerve gas attack on the Tokyo subway system in 1995. Some of the key people who participated in that horrific event were ordinary Japanese citizens who allowed their desire for spiritual enlightenment to lead them into the lair of a monster. Unfortunately, there can be somewhat of a cold materialism on the surface of western civilization and many people never learn how to penetrate beyond that surface. Lost and alone, these folks are prime targets for radicals acting in the name of one cause or another.

All across the world, Islamic fundamentalists claim to have the answers to life and many people have bought what they sell. In their recruiting message, these deceitful fanatics use the time honored tactic of blaming the problems of the Islamic world on someone else. "Everything is the fault of the West" they say. "Were it not for the Great Satan (United States), all would be well in our world." With simple statements and a willingness to back up their words with actions they are able to appeal to a large number of people.

Organizations have played this evil game for centuries. One of the best ways to control people is to get them focused on something outside their daily life. Something that they can blame for their problems. With Adolph Hitler, it was the Jews. With the Communists, it was western capitalism and the rich, and with some of our own characters it has been economic factors or perceived racism. Get the attention of the down-trodden or oppressed and tell them that you have found the "boogie-man," and you can get some of them to do just about anything. That the problems of a society or people in question may be more of their own making than that of someone else is something that you will never hear mentioned in this game, even though that is more than likely the truth of the matter. Today, radical Islam is playing this game all over the world and playing it well. Whether or not their success will continue is something that we will have to wait and see.

Every day, more and more people want to jump up and tell you and me that the radicals of Islam do not represent the majority of the practitioners of that faith. "Most of these are peaceful people," they tell us, "just wanting to go about life like everyone else." In other words, the radicals among them do not represent them all. Therefore, we should not judge the many by the actions of a few. Well friends, that is probably true, but there needs to be a bit more detail added to the equation. I will concede that the overwhelming majority of Muslims are normal peaceful people and do not directly support the radicals. Be that as it may, you need to realize a few other facts. For many people, Islam is not so much a religion as it is an indoctrination. If a given person was raised in this belief, he or she will be bound to that belief for life. No matter the actions of the radicals, the devoted will cling to their religion. For many Muslims, allegiance to this faith means a part of them ideologically supports the Jihadists. These individuals may never admit this fact and they may never go as far as to actually take part in an attack but, they will emotionally embrace the terrorists and their cause. In a verbal confrontation these persons will make endless excuses for the mayhem and those who perpetrate it. The bad ones hide among the good ones and that is the way of things all across the globe.

It is important to remember that the peaceful ones will not protect you from the violent ones.

The creation of the Arab States

"The dreamers of the day are dangerous men for they may act their dream with open eyes and make it possible."

Thomas Edward Lawrence ("Lawrence of Arabia")

British officer, First World War

Islam may be an old religion, but the Islamic Arab world as you see it today has not existed for long. Prior to the First World War, that part of the world consisted of scattered tribal units that fought each other for control of small areas. For the most part, the national boundaries that we know today did not exist, nor did the national identities that go with them. The Arab world that you see today was almost entirely a creation of the western powers of that time. The chickens that are coming home to roost were hatched a long time ago.

In 1919, with the end of the First World War, the Allied powers stood victorious. They had totally defeated their enemies and the spoils were theirs. Along with much of the European continent, they had conquered the Arab world as it existed at that time. That world was theirs to do with as they wished. Even at that early age of industrial development, these powers could clearly see the potential represented by the enormous reserves of oil that lay beneath all that sand. They concluded that they had better get a handle on the situation or others would. So they set about carving up the Arab World to suit their needs.

From a vast region of unorganized tribes, these powers set about creating a collection of nationalities set on the European model. They simply invented countries and forced them into existence. Prior to this time there was no such thing as the nations of Jordan, Kuwait, or even Saudi Arabia. One day they did not exist and the next day they did. These areas became de-facto nations and were expected to function as such. That the inhabitants of these areas may have other ideas was something that evidently did not occur to the nation builders of the day.

An eastern tribal culture carries with it a set of values that is in total opposition to western national culture. The two are completely incompatible, and only with the passage of many generations can the tribal outlook surrender to the national one. Nowhere near has the necessary number of generations passed for this change to occur in the region. As a result, what we have today are large populations of the area that have a national identity in name only. A person from those locations may call themselves a Jordanian, or a Kuwaiti, or a Saudi Arabian. When they do, it is usually for the benefit of their interaction with a westerner. Inside, many of them still identify themselves as a member of the tribal group from which they originated. The potential problems that may arise from this set of circumstances should be obvious, yet the western world still wonders why they don't think or act like us. To be fair, it must be pointed out that the United States actually had little to do with the makeover of that region, and argued against much of it as it was happening. Unfortunately, no one was inclined to listen, so we are stuck dealing with the situation in modern times.

Of all the tribal baggage that these societies kept, none carried as much weight as their religion: Islam. The shift from a tribal structure to national one did not dilute this influence in the least and in fact, the influence of Islam was probably strengthened during this time. The residents of the Arab world during that era were suddenly thrust into the twentieth century without opportunity to catch their breath or even begin to understand the changes around them. Faced with these circumstances, the people of this time clung even tighter to what was known. That brings us to today.

The modern Arab World

"Hatred is a feeling which leads to the extinction of values."

Jose Ortega Gasset

Spanish philosopher

The Arab nations of today have been involved in the creation and spread of Islamic terrorism since their inception. They have always directly or indirectly supported this evil, and they probably always will. There are both cultural and practical reasons for this situation. On the cultural side of the issue, Arab governments support terror because a significant percentage of the individuals in government service in those nations ideologically agree with the terrorist cause. They set about supporting the ideas of radical Islam because they believe in those ideals. Islam is the religion of their birth and they have been indoctrinated in that faith all of their lives. Unlike their western counterparts, these folks have no mental ability to subjugate their faith in favor of their day-to-day responsibilities. The Taliban movement in Afghanistan was brought into existence by Pakistani intelligence officers. Once in power, this organization operated as the military, police force, economic council, and religious platform for the nation. Obviously, there is no secular separation of church and state in their world.

On the practical side of the issue, Arab governments support terrorism because they are at any given time in mortal danger of being overthrown by the proponents of that terrorism. Radical Islam permeates their societies and continuously riles the masses against the existing power structures. These governments have all had to make concessions with the radicals among them in order to stay in theoretical control. One of the biggest concessions they have made is to turn over the educational system in their nation to the religious extremists.

As you read this book, thousands of children in the Arab world are being indoctrinated into a level of animalistic hatred that defies comprehension. Generations of youths have been told that all of the failings of their society are not the fault of the structure of that society or the shortcomings of those who lead it. Instead, they have been told that all the ills in their world are totally the fault of the West and, in particular, the United States of America. Their hatred for you and me is all encompassing because they have been immersed in that malice all of their lives. They have never met you or me and probably never will. All they same they have been taught that our society and its influence is the cause of all of their misery and they will not hesitate to kill either you or me. These people are poorly educated by western standards, and largely ignorant of the world around them. The only thing that they see of us is what the radicals who control them want them to see. Unfortunately, our society tends to play into the hands of these religious zealots. The only section of our culture that is routinely displayed to them are the products of our sick and twisted entertainment industry.

What would you think?

"Airing one's dirty linen never makes for a masterpiece."

Francois Truffaut

French screenwriter

Imagine that you are a person from another culture and the only thing that you know about the United States of America is what you had gathered from watching one of our many movies or television shows. What would your opinion of us be then? What would you think of this nation if the only window of information that you had was modern "Gangsta Rap" music? After a few hours of listening to some drug dealing thug howl about the joys of murder, sexual assault, and thievery, what would be your impression of the society that created and exported that? If you were from a culture that considered marriage and family life to be something honorable and sacred, what would your opinion be after a few hours of "Married with Children," "Desperate Housewives," or "Sex in the City"? If you came from a society that considered sexual modesty to be in the best interest of all, what would you think after a few episodes of "Howard Stern" or "Music Television"? Forget about the shows and movies, what would you think if the only thing that you knew about us came from our television commercials? Personally, I would imagine that a few hours spent watching child-like imbeciles flit about the screen selling useless things, would be enough to influence anyone's point of view in the negative.

You and I both know that Hollywood and the television industry do not represent the United States of America and its cultural values. At least, I hope you know that. We know that this nation is made up of decent people who have little in common with this small part of our society. We know that this is just entertainment, sick and twisted though it is, and not the totality of our civilization. Be that as it may, many of the people in the world of Islam do not know this and they will never know it. They will never know it because the radicals in control of them are not going to let them know it. They use this aspect of our society against us every single day and they will continue to do so. Islam is an ancient religion, but the modern radical element among them have discovered a weaknesses in our culture and learned how to use it against us. Think about that the next time you turn on the television and dive into the insanity.

The Arab-Israeli Situation

"He who lives by fighting with an enemy has an interest in the preservation of the enemies' life."

Nietzsche

19th century German philosopher

As I finished this book I turned forty-seven years old. For all of you youngsters who are reading this, I have some shocking and disturbing news. Boys and girls, there was a time when the Internet did not exist. There were no personal computers and even the electronic calculator had not yet appeared. Most horrible of all, there was no such thing as cable or satellite television. Television, as we knew it then, was a bit different than today. I remember when my father bought our first set in 1968. It was a used black and white model, and I only mention the black and white aspect because there was almost no affordable option for color. It was not particularly big, and the picture quality would not even begin to meet today's standards. If you wanted to receive a particular station, you had to manually adjust a small antenna on top of the set. Even more horrifying was the fact that there was no such thing as a remote control. That's right, youngsters; if you wanted to change channels or adjust the volume you had to raise yourself out of the down position and do it by hand. Unthinkable, I realize, and how we managed to survive such inhumane conditions remains a mystery. Still, for all its shortcomings by today's standards, it was a miracle of modern technology. For the first time ever, we, the average American citizens, had a window on the world. Every night we could watch the NBC, ABC, or CBS nightly news and get a look at what was going on around the globe. Every once in a while, it was even live for about ten seconds. From that time until now, I don't remember a day that I could not turn on my television set and watch Arabs and Jews going about the business of killing each other. Oh, they would take a break now and then, but they always got right back to the fight. One asks when will it end, and I am afraid that the correct answer is "probably never." It appears that the world is going to be stuck with this situation for a long time.

The Arab-Israeli situation began with the emigration of large numbers of European Jews to the Middle East in the aftermath of the Second World War. These were the survivors of the Nazi concentration camps and it is easy to understand why they would have wanted to leave the place that gave them such a horrific experience. These people had come to the conclusion that only in a nation comprised of their own kind, could they enjoy physical security from the world around them. They determined that the location of this new nation was to be their ancient biblical homeland; then called Palestine. Understandable as their sentiment was, it did not take into account the fact that the area was already occupied.

Friction between the new settlers and the long time residents began immediately. Absentee landlords (mostly Syrians or Ottoman Turks) sold large tracts of supposedly worthless land to emigrating

Jews, putting them literally across the road from their Arab neighbors. The Jewish settlers quickly proved that the land was not worthless and was quite valuable with the appropriate amount of real work. The results were inevitable. On one side of the road was an apathetic tribal culture that owned none of the land that it occupied and felt no compulsion to make it better. On the other side was an industrious and purpose driven people who had recently survived a session of genocide. This situation brought anger and resentment from one direction and contempt and derision from the other. It was not long before the first shots were fired.

The situation exploded into all out war with the Israeli declaration of independence in May of 1948. Prior to this, the fighting had primarily been between Jewish settlers and Palestinian insurgents. This declaration brought all of the surrounding Arab nations into the conflict and the modern situation was created. In preparation for their coming invasion, the Arab nations of Egypt, Syria, Jordan, and others persuaded large numbers of Palestinian civilians to needlessly flee their lands in the advance of this incursion. For reasons of self-interest, arrogance, and laziness, both the Arabs and the Jews have allowed this exile to become a permanent situation.

The Israeli declaration of independence began an era of non-stop conventional warfare with their Arab neighbors. As the decades passed, the conflicts arose again and again. In 1954-56 there was the "War of Attrition" and the Suez Canal Crisis. In 1967 came the "Six Day War" in which the Israelis were able to inflict such a catastrophic defeat on their enemies that their national survival was temporarily assured. Then in 1973 came the "War of Atonement," or as it is known in that region, the "Yom Kippur War." In this conflict, the Arab Armies, equipped with modern Soviet weaponry, came within a few kilometers of cutting the nation of Israel in half. The Jewish state was saved in the last hours by a massive re-supply operation from the United States that allowed her army to stay in the fight. In 1982, wishing to rid themselves of a guerrilla threat, the Israelis invaded their northern neighbor, Lebanon. This operation culminated with the capture of Beirut and the crushing defeat of the Syrian Army in the Bekka Valley.

In the aftermath of the Syrian defeat, most of the nations surrounding Israel came to the realization that they were not capable of militarily defeating the Jewish state. They had decimated their economies and sacrificed tens of thousands of their citizens for no return. Israel was there to stay and, one by one, they began to accept this fact. The decade of the eighties saw the beginning of a peace process between these nations and the State of Israel. Egypt was first, and then followed Jordan and Syria. All these countries have signed peace treaties with the Jewish nation and these documents have signaled an end to the era of conventional military conflict in the region. There have been no more massive armored and aerial battles fought in the Sinai Desert or the Golan Heights. There have been some large scale skirmishes, such as the fighting in southern Lebanon in 2006, and repeats of this are probably in our future. That aside, peace has (for the most part) been declared and the big wars are probably over. On the other hand, the killing and destruction has continued and will continue for the foreseeable future.

Rather than trying to defeat the Israelis with tanks and jet fighters, the Arab nations of the region turned to supporting the Palestinian resistance groups in Israel. This support has resulted in a series of bloody uprisings by these groups that continues into the present day. The suicide bomber has taken the place of the Soviet T-64 tank and Mig-21 fighter jet. For the past few years, we have turned on our television sets and witnessed the smoking ruins of buses and restaurants. Streets are filled with dazed survivors as the ambulances shriek in the background. Politicians on both sides of the conflict babble about peace while the carnage continues.

Again the question is asked "when will this situation end?" I am not capable of answering that question and I have not heard from anyone who can. Unfortunately, this situation may be something that the human race is stuck with for the foreseeable future. There may be no end possible in our lifetimes. Both sides of this struggle have a vested interest in seeing it continue. For the Palestinian resistance groups, non-stop bloodshed means survival as an organization and continued influence over the population of the area. For the Israelis, non-stop bloodshed means that they are perceived by the American people to be a stranded outpost of western culture surrounded by vicious enemies. This perception assures them billions of dollars per year from the U.S. Treasury.

The Arab world believes that the United States has wholeheartedly sided with the Israelis in this conflict. If you talk to the man in the street in that region, this will be the complaint that will surface most often. This may have once been true, but it is true no longer. Over the last decade, the power and influence of the "Israeli lobby" in this country has fallen and it is still falling. On the fiscal side of the issue, we give as much money to the Arabs as we do to the Israelis. So it can no longer be said that we favor one side over the other. That is simply no longer the truth. True or not, the belief of the average Arab citizen in that region continues to be that the United States is a single minded ally of Israel and only Israel. The chances of changing their minds on this issue are not promising.

Osama and the Al Qaeda

"Hostility toward America is a religious duty, and we hope to be rewarded for it by God...I am confident that Muslims will be able to end the legend of the so-called superpower that is America."

Osama bin Laden

Al Qaeda leader

Prior to the attacks of 9/11, few Americans had ever heard of Osama bin Laden and the organization that he founded. Of those who were aware of his presence, even fewer realized the grave threat that he represented to their nation and culture. Now he is a household word and you would be hard pressed to find someone who does not know *who* he is. On the other hand, I think that you could easily find people who do not know *what* he is. Osama bin Laden and the Al Qaeda network is the main enemy that we face in the War on Terror. Osama is Saudi Arabian by nationality and so is most of his inner circle. Al Qaeda means "the base' or "the foundation" in Arabic. It is a loose affiliation of like-minded Islamic terror groups worldwide. One of the mistakes that people in our culture make when they visualize the enemy is that they try to see him in our image. A lot of people visualize a western style, James Bond like organization with a well organized command structure. That set of circumstances does not exist because their culture will not allow it. They have a de-centralized structure and do not follow a western model of organization. There are many radical Islamic individuals and organizations that claim to be a part of the Al Qaeda but are not connected directly to Osama. These organizations are still part of the problem because of their ideological alignment.

Osama and the Al Qaeda have some ties to the Arab-Israeli situation and will use that situation for propaganda purposes if it suits them. The reality is, however, that they don't really care about that situation or those in it. In his ranting and ravings Osama only rarely mentions that conflict. He and his organization have much bigger fish to fry than a regional war. These folks are engaged in what they see as a face-off between the World of Islam and the twenty-first century West. It is an ideological struggle for the future of that region and, to a degree, the human race. They have a vision of a glorious Islamic Empire consisting of all Muslim countries united under a single leader. In their mind this empire will compete with the west economically, militarily, and culturally, and they will do this while being ruled by a thought process straight out of the sixth century. Now, you and I understand that this arrangement could not happen. We can look at the logic of it and see the truth. They, on the other hand, feel no obligation to base things on fact or logic and prefer to stick to the fantasy. This is not a new situation and radical Muslims have held this vision for centuries. These people look at the modern western world and see the progress that has been made. They then have to make a comparison to the situation existing in their own civilizations. In general, the Islamic world lags far behind the west in cultural and economic development, and the evidence of this is inescapable. This comparison serves to arouse jealousy and resentment and a desire to destroy that with which they cannot compete.

As logical thinking westerners, we can look at the beliefs of these people and see the contradictions and impossibilities. They, on the other hand, can never do that. They have no ability to be introspective and we need not hold our breaths waiting for them to develop that ability. In any event, it's not important. The important thing is to remember that they will absolutely never quit. They will never change their mind about the situation and their role in it. They will continue the fight as long as they are able to do so. Delusional or not, the Al Qaeda is far more dangerous and well organized than any of the insurgent groups involved in the Arab-Israeli situation. They bitterly resent the influence of the western world, particularly the United States, on their populations and will do anything to end that influence. They fear that the ingress of western ideas will erode the power of the Islam. In their minds, that erosion will cause Islam to lose its place as the single controlling factor over the lives of the people in the region. This is a situation that they will not tolerate. They will do whatever it takes to maintain their hold on the people and the region because they know that if they lose it, they will never get it back.

In a nutshell, that is the state of affairs. In just a few pages I have probably given you more real information than the politicians or television newscasters have for the last several years of your life. Having said all of that, you must also realize that this is not the totality of the situation and many more words have been written about the subject. For that reason alone, I would encourage my fellow citizens to dig even deeper. Knowledge is power and the best way to gain that knowledge is to find it yourself. That knowledge is there if you want it.

Chapter 3

The Organization of Terror

"Their poison is like the poison of a serpent."

Bible: Psalm 58:4

For the first time since the Second World War we face an enemy that is capable of defeating us. This is a war that we can lose if we are not careful. Will we wake up one morning to see Osama's fighters marching down our streets? No, they don't possess the material or mindset to project conventional force on any scale that could harm us. That type of warfare has always been our game, not theirs. They are not capable of physically conquering us, yet they can still win this war.

What they are capable of doing is striking our economy and social fabric such a serious blow that it would begin to collapse and life, as we know it, would come to a stop. This enemy could launch a series of attacks that would so damage the infrastructure upon which we rely, that it will no longer support us. These attacks could also spread fear on such a scale that our society will lose confidence and turn on itself. All this they would do, if we let them. As we go about our daily existence, the veneer of civilization and comfort surrounds us. I call it a veneer because that is exactly what it is. It is without real substance and very thin, indeed. As long as today looks more or less like yesterday and we have confidence that tomorrow will be the same, everything is fine. If that confidence goes away, civilization goes with it. We have had a recent example of just how quickly it can go away.

The situation that developed in the city of New Orleans and surrounding area in the aftermath of Hurricane Katrina reveals just how thin the covering is. Within a few hours an ordinary American city disintegrated in medieval chaos. Bodies floated in the streets while buildings burned around them. Gangs of murderous thugs roamed the city, killing and robbing at will. Tens of thousands of citizens gathered in a sports arena and convention center and sat helplessly, waiting to be rescued. The police department was shattered by desertions and outside agencies struggled to get the situation under control. There was no food, no water, no hospitals that were not flooded beyond capacity, and no electricity. The economic base of the city was destroyed and it will take years to repair, if indeed it ever is.

In the towns surrounding New Orleans, the physical destruction from the storm was fairly light. The overall situation, however, was just as severe. Inundated by hundreds of thousands of refugees, these population centers ceased to function normally and every day life came to a halt. There was no gas in the pumps, no food in the stores, and no way to know what the future was going to be. All this was taking place in summertime conditions in Louisiana during a period of record heat and humidity. As the hours passed, tempers grew short and panic began to set in. Life as it was known before the hurricane had ceased to exist.

The situation in New Orleans was brought about by an act of nature, rather than an act of terror. That is the only real difference that I see. All of the results that we saw, and are continuing to see, would be the same in a massive terrorist attack. If the Al Qaeda can launch a coordinated series of attacks on several cities at once, they may permanently shatter that veneer. The economy may be so weakened from the destruction of the attacks and the loss of confidence by the citizenry that it may never fully recover.

To accomplish this goal, the enemy must be able to infiltrate our society and move among us. He must have the ability to transfer money, materials, and people from one location to another, relatively unobserved. He has to have organization and structure in the places that he intends to attack and these assets have to be in place before the event.

The organization of a terrorist group

In order to survive in a hostile environment a terrorist group must break down into sub structures or cells. If they did not take this precaution the capture of a single individual would place the entire organization in jeopardy. As I describe the basic setup, keep in mind that there are endless variations possible to this structure and the Al Qaeda is not obligated to prefer one over another. Their basic organization will consist of logistical cells, reconnaissance cells, and attack cells. All of these small groups will be under the control of a single agent or mission commander.

The logistical cell provides all of the material needs of the group involved in the operation. This cell will probably be made up of local citizens or resident aliens who have been in the United States long enough to assimilate into our culture. They may be people who have been here for several generations and are indistinguishable from the average citizen other than by ethnic features. They may speak perfect American English and be able to navigate through day-to-day life in this society with ease. These individuals will probably not associate with radical organizations and may not even attend the mosque regularly. They may be involved in petty crimes such as Internet fraud or credit card thievery in order to raise money for their organization. They may be business owners and make sandwiches or dry clean clothes by day. Some of them will have the material assets necessary to temporarily support the preparation of an attack. These assets will include transportation and housing for others who will be brought in to carry out the operation.

These folks live in your town and you probably see them on a regular basis. They will appear harmless and, in most circumstances, they are. They may have never had actual contact with the more hardened members and may never participate in an actual event. They may only carry the ideological willingness to participate and that is enough. In most cases, these people will not be fully trusted by the involved organization and may not be aware of the operation at all.

Members of a reconnaissance cell may look identical to those in the logistical cell, but they will be different people. These members may be locals or people from outside, but they will have more training and the trust of the organization involved. These folks will do the looking and gather intelligence for the attack. They will be well equipped with digital photography equipment and computers. They know what they are looking for and how to go about gathering the information in a more or less clandestine manner. They will probably not be hardened fighters but they may have some combat experience. They will only interact with the logistics cell if it is absolutely necessary. The presence of a reconnaissance cell does not necessarily mean that an attack is imminent. They could simply be on a fact-finding mission.

The individuals who make up the attack or operational cell are the *real deal*. These individuals will probably be hardened fighters and may have a significant amount of combat experience. They will probably come to the United States from somewhere else and will only be on the ground for the amount of time absolutely necessary to complete the operation. These people possess a lot of critical information that could be harmful to the organization if they are captured, so they will be exposed for the shortest time possible. If you confront one of these people you are facing a genuine "natural born killer." At that moment, you have both feet in a grave and a shovel in your hand. Trust me on this folks, they will not hesitate to murder you or anyone around you if they feel such action is necessary. In fact, some of them will kill you just because the opportunity presented itself. If you are a police officer, you may be mere seconds away from the gunfight of your career. One moment you are writing a traffic ticket and the next moment you are in an infantry battle in the dark. I'm not trying to be dramatic here, just truthful. Remember, these folks have been in places where the U.S. Army hunts them at night with M-1 tanks and Apache helicopters. Even if they managed to survive the technological threat, they have had to contend with onslaughts by hundreds of American infantrymen who are just as proficient in killing as they are. If they are still alive after a few of those encounters, they have learned some hard lessons and can be relied upon to make no mistakes.

Additionally, the operation that they are on may be a suicide mission. If that is the case, they know that they are riding a one-way ticket to a virgin-infested paradise and will have no attack of conscience when it comes to killing you or anyone as unfortunate enough as to be in their path. The individuals that comprise an attack cell will be generally proficient with weapons although this skill will vary from individual to individual. Actual skill aside, many of them will be perfectly willing to use those weapons if the opportunity arises. Many of them will fight to the death if cornered and will not hesitate to add innocent bystanders to their score. Remember, these folks think that they are working for God and they want to make him proud.

The controlling agent or mission commander is the linchpin for the entire operation. Of all the members of the organization, he will be the most invisible and will possess the most impeccable credentials. He will probably work in a white-collar occupation and will have lived or traveled in the West for many years. This individual is responsible for setting up and carrying out the attack. All of the involved cells will have contact with this person; so, in a way, he is the weak link. If he is threatened or captured, the operation will be finished. If you are a member of the law enforcement community and you ever think that you have one of these guys, shut him down. Make him unable to contact the rest of his personnel and the operation will probably fizzle out. If nothing else, convince him that you know all about the plan and he will probably pull the plug.

Capabilities of a terrorist group

When it comes to carrying out an attack on U.S. soil, a terrorist group is only limited by their imagination and ability. One of the things that makes the Al Qaeda so dangerous is that it is comprised of many different groups with no real command and control. An Al Qaeda affiliated group can launch an attack either on order or by their own volition. There may be no stream of message traffic or intelligence to warn us of an impending operation. Whatever their origins, the thing to keep in mind is that the goal of a terrorist group is to inflict death and destruction upon their enemies. They will set about to accomplish this task by different means. These means include, but are not limited to, assassinations, kidnappings, bombings, and attacks with weapons of mass destruction.

Prior to 9/11, the assassination of specific individuals is something that the Al Qaeda had, more or less, reserved for their own. Since 9/11, they have ventured into the arena of murdering individual westerners foolish enough to be wandering about in countries of that region. They have also targeted western government officials in some of their operations. I personally would not look for this to become a common trend. The target of a single individual takes the same level of commitment and risk that would be required for an attack on a group. Unless the victim is a person of popularity or political prominence, there is little return for that risk. They have done it in their part of the world for the simple reason that they can operate more freely in that area. To conduct the same type of operation on U.S. soil would be much more difficult, but, by no means impossible.

The kidnapping of a specific individual has become a routine activity on the part of terrorist organizations worldwide. They conduct this type of operation because it has paid off for them, literally. Kidnapping a person for ransom or political pressure is almost guaranteed to have positive results for the group that carries it out. Millions of dollars are fed into terrorist group coffers as the ransoms are paid for the return of the kidnapped individuals. If the payment is refused, the terrorist group will still have the satisfaction of brutally murdering the victim, which is probably what they had in mind in the first place. Kidnapping works for the terrorist group because, for the last three decades, the western world has taught them that it works. It is part of our cultural make-up to value life and we will usually take whatever steps are necessary to recover and preserve life. We have paid off again and again and then sat around wondering why the kidnappings continue. Only recently has the United States attempted to reverse this trend by refusing to bargain for kidnap victims in Iraq. That is a positive step but, as this conflict intensifies, we will see whether it continues.

The bomb has long been the favorite toy of the terrorist group and over seventy percent of attacks worldwide are some sort of bombing incident. Like kidnapping, the terrorists use this method because history has taught them that it works. Unlike a direct attack, bombing operations are relatively inexpensive and carry a reduced risk for the group involved. All that is necessary is to manufacture the device, place the device, and detonate the device. Their lack of concern for collateral damage or the death of bystanders makes this type of attack even easier to carry out. Ordinary bombings are bad enough, but there has been a new method employed by terrorist groups over the last two decades that has made this type of attack more terrifying: the suicide bomber

The suicide bomber is not a new invention and this method of warfare has been used throughout history. In the Second World War the appearance of the Japanese Kamikaze pilot in the Pacific theater of operations initially came as a shock to the American forces. The thought of someone deliberately plunging to their death was a concept that was hard for us to grasp in the beginning. We figured it out quickly enough, and the main lesson that we learned during that time was to not let this type of attack deter us from our goal. Some of this lesson has been retained and we don't seem to be willing to allow this sort of attack to deter us from our goals in Iraq or elsewhere oversees. Be that as it may, the suicide bomber has not shown up here, yet. The day he does show up is the day that we will learn what level of resolve actually exists in our society.

Weapons of Mass Destruction

"And I looked and beheld a pale horse: and his name that sat on him was Death"

Bible: Revelations 6:8

The term Weapons of Mass Destruction (or WMD) has become a household word in the United States since 9/11. The threat of these weapons was the stated reason for our invasion of Iraq and billions of dollars are spent every year training and preparing for this type of attack. The possibilities are indeed horrifying to contemplate, and we all should pray that it never happens. There are some aspects of this issue, however, that require a closer examination if we are to fully understand the threat. Weapons of Mass Destruction break down into the following categories: chemical, biological, radiological, nuclear, and explosive, or CBRNE for short. Incendiaries were recently added to the list, and 9/11 was actually an incendiary attack. Each one of these is a possibility if the terrorists can gather the personnel and equipment necessary to carry it out. On the other hand, there are inherent difficulties and consequences that go with the use of these weapons.

In a chemical scenario, the terrorist group disperses a deadly toxin to a specific target or a large area. Incidents involving crop-dusting aircraft spraying a chemical or biological agent over a large area have been visualized by federal law enforcement and jabbered about by the news media. In reality, the operation may not rely on a specific delivery device and instead may be as simple as the terrorist group causing a massive leak on a vessel carrying the agent. The derailment of a freight train or the grounding of a sea-going vessel would meet these ends. If the operation were successful, the results would be ugly. There would be deaths and injuries in the affected area and the resulting panic of the affected population would probably be worse. In fact, this scenario has already happened.

The March 20, 1995, nerve gas attack against the Tokyo subway system shows us that this type of operation is well within the capability of a terrorist group. This operation was a model of simplicity and non-complication. The perpetrators boarded different subway trains, each carrying liquid SARIN (nerve agent) in zip-lock bags. At a pre-determined location, each terrorist simply dropped his bag onto the floor of the car and punctured it with the sharpened tip of an umbrella. This action was timed to coincide with a stop so that the terrorist could rapidly depart the car as he deployed the weapon. The results of these attacks were twelve dead and several thousands injured, most of them severely. The reason that the results were not worse was due to the relatively low purity of the SARIN liquid that was used. Had the terrorists been equipped with a purer form of the weapon, the casualties would have been in the hundreds of thousands; the damage to the Japanese economy may have been unrecoverable. When compared to a biological or nuclear scenario, the chemical attack is probably the easiest task for a terrorist group to accomplish. There is still much difficulty and risk to those involved, however. The storage and transportation of a deadly chemical is something that is quite difficult and threatens the lives of those doing it. Even something as simple as a train derailment brings no guarantee of success and may wipe out the perpetrators of the act.

Of all of the WMD possibilities, it is the biological attack that conjures up the most fear in the general public. The rest of the scenarios can be difficult for the average citizen to visualize but everyone knows what it feels like to be sick. In this situation, a terrorist group disperses a weaponized bacteria or virus throughout an area, hoping that enough people will be infected to spread it to the larger population. When enough people are infected, the results could be the stuff of nightmares. If enough people get sick, die, or are quarantined, society will come to a stop and may not be able to continue again. One of the biggest dangers that we face in this type of attack is the lack of warning. Even a weaponized germ will take time to affect the population and the early signs of the outbreak may be mistaken for normal sickness patterns in the population. It may be weeks or months before we know that we are under attack or have any idea of where it originated.

Horrible as this scenario is, it presents real problems for the terrorist. In order to produce the weaponized germ, he has to have access to the necessary laboratory facilities and the personnel who know how to grow the disease. This usually means that the terrorist must seek the help of a friendly government and that situation is getting harder to come by. Once the weapon is created, it must then be transported to the target location and dispersed in some manner. The success or failure of the dispersal will not be known for quite some time. If the dispersal is unsuccessful, the terrorist must try again or go on to something else. If the attack is successful, then the terrorist knows that the sickness will reach his homeland eventually. The sheer volume of air travel around the planet would guarantee a global infection, sooner or later.

When it comes to nuclear weapons, things are no less complicated for the terrorist. In this scenario, there is a choice between an actual nuclear weapon and what is known as a Radiological Dispersal Device or RDD. An RDD is also referred to as a "dirty bomb" and is nothing more than low grade radioactive material wrapped around a conventional explosive. Upon detonation, the contaminated material is dispersed throughout the area of the blast. The effectiveness of this type of attack depends on several factors. These include the amount of explosive, the level of radioactivity in the material, and the wind patterns in the area of the blast. If the terrorist is successful with this type of attack, then the short-term destruction may be far overshadowed by the long-term radiological contamination of a large area. If such a strike is carried out in the central business district of a major city, then the downtown area could be shut down, literally, for decades. All of the critical items in that area, such as critical documents and money would be lost. The resulting economic effects could be catastrophic.

Potentially bad as this could be, the terrorist is still up against some real problems. His body cannot withstand the brutal effects of a large dose of deadly radiation any more than yours can. If he chooses to follow this path, then he will have some major hoops to jump through. He has to procure the deadly material and keep it in a safe configuration until he assembles his weapon. When he assembles the weapon, he must un-shield the material and co-locate it with the conventional explosives. Should he manage to do this action quickly, he will still be exposed to the effects of the radiation.

The other side of this possibility is a fission detonation of an actual nuclear device. This has long been considered to be the least likely but most potentially destructive type of attack in the WMD scenario. If such a weapon were deployed in a major population center, then that city would literally cease to exist. The destruction would be on an unimaginable scale and the area would be unsafe to re-enter for many years. Radiation sickness would kill as many people as the initial blast. Sickness and birth defects would be carried into the following generations. This would be a horror show of the greatest magnitude.

If the terrorist chooses to initiate an actual nuclear detonation, then his path becomes a hard one. He must either acquire or manufacture an atomic bomb and transport that weapon to the desired target. I know that Hollywood would have you believe that any person of ordinary intelligence can manufacture a working nuclear weapon in their garage. According to them, all that is needed is a belligerent attitude, combined with a couple of trips to Home Depot and Radio Shack, and you're in business. Like a lot of information that comes from this medium, this is not true. An atomic bomb is one of the most technologically complicated devices ever invented. In the sequence of detonation, several dozen events must take place with an accuracy of billionths of a second. That's billionths with a B. If anything gets out of place during this sequence, there will be no big bang. That level of technology cannot be produced in a garage. Therefore, if the terrorist chooses to build such a device then he is up against the same problems that arose with the weaponized biological substance. He must have sufficient laboratory assets and the people to run them. This will probably mean the involvement of some nation friendly to the terrorist cause. While this is certainly a possibility, the potential for massive U.S. retaliation against that government makes this scenario an unlikely one.

Could the terrorist simply lay hands on some piece of pre-manufactured military nuclear ordinance, most likely from the former Soviet Union, and carry out his attack with this ready-made weapon? Obviously the answer is yes, but there are still some problems. As one of the most technologically complicated devices known to man, an atomic bomb is also one of the most maintenance-dependent devices in the arsenal. You cannot hide one of these things in a cave in Afghanistan for twenty years and be sure that it will work. This problem will again lead the terrorist to seeking a friendly government to provide him with the weapon. If such a government were to so equip a terrorist organization, and an attack was actually carried out on U.S. soil, then that government would be in line for horrific retribution. Our actions in Iraq have shown the world just how seriously we take the threat of these weapons and what we are willing to do in order to protect ourselves from them. Faced with this threat, we will not hesitate to kill large numbers of people and the world is starting to realize this fact.

The Suicide Bomber

"It was always my wish to turn my body into deadly shrapnel"

Reem al-Reyashi, (age 22, mother of two)

Female Palestinian suicide bomber

Of all the potential threats that can be used by a terrorist group operating in our midst, this is the most worrisome. In this scenario, the terrorist cell recruits a number of potential bombers, indoctrinates them, and sets them loose on an unsuspecting community. It's a simple process logistically as well: no laboratories, no complicated transportation or delivery issues, just send the bomber to the desired target and blow him up. Even if the physical damage were light in comparison to what would be suffered in a more exotic WMD attack, the psychological impact would be comparable or worse.

At eight o'clock in the morning a suicide bomber climbs aboard a city transit bus in your city or town, He is a second or third

40

generation American citizen, so nothing sets him apart, other than his ethnic features (and we have been long-indoctrinated against the idea of noticing that, haven't we?) He speaks American English and wears the latest style of clothes, including the ever-present backpack. He may not even know that he is on a one-way ride, as the suicide bombers of the future may be unaware of the reality they are facing. The terrorist group that recruited him may not have informed him of the true nature of his mission and, therefore, he is not even a suicide bomber in the truest sense of the term. He may think that he is performing some more mundane task for the group and will show none of the psychological signs, such as nervousness or sweating, normally associated with this kind of threat.

At a pre-determined time and place the bomber's device is detonated, more than likely by remote control. One second there is a bus hissing to a stop and in the next instant, a thunderous explosion accompanied by fire and smoke. As the sound of the explosion fades there is a few seconds of silent shock and then the screaming begins. The screaming continues even as the wail of sirens begins to be heard in the background. As the first responders arrive, a nightmarish scene greets them. The bus is partially disintegrated and the vehicle has been rendered unrecognizable. Glass, debris, and body parts have been slung about for hundreds of feet and the dazed survivors wander though this mess looking for those who were just with them a couple of moments ago.

As the next few hours pass, the true nature of the attack may not be known and may not be immediately released to the public, if it is known. Word of the incident will travel fast, however, and fear and uncertainty will already be pervasive. If it is a single incident, then the fear will only reach a certain level. Relatively few people will be physically affected and most of the effect will be psychological. The community will be in shock and dismay, and the political fallout will be enormous nationwide, but the effected area will eventually return to normal. If other bombings follow the initial attack, then it is a different story. If the attacks continue, perhaps at different locations such as a crowded shopping mall or movie theater, then the structure of the affected society will disintegrate.

If the attacks continue into the next day, that society will cease to exist in any recognizable form. Daily life would halt in its tracks. No one would go to work or put their children on the school bus. Terror and uncertainty would be the order of the day and chaos would reign. Law enforcement, fire departments, and the medical service institutions would find themselves overwhelmed by the incidents and their effectiveness would fade. Retaliatory vigilante attacks would be conducted against the Islamic population in the area, adding to the fear and mistrust. The mess would eventually be cleaned up, but life would never be the same.

Another aspect of the terrorist threat that is being overlooked on both a national and local level is the copycat. This is a second or third generation youth that has been raised in an American Islamic household and is open for recruitment by the radicals. While speculation suggests that such a group may not have quite the destructive capabilities of a well trained foreign cell, they cannot be discounted. One of the problems would be the absence of an international signature that can be recognized by our national intelligence services. An operation carried out at the local level will give no warning in the form of international e-mail or telephone calls. The recent arrest of the youths in Miami who were allegedly plotting to blow up the Sears Tower in Chicago supports this possibility. As time passes, the threat may come more from within than without.

The Weaknesses of a Terrorist Group.

The Al Qaeda has its strengths; that much is obvious. This dispersed, loosely-knit group has the capacity to bring much death and suffering into our lives and they have proven this on many occasions. The reminders of this fact are presented to us almost daily. However, that is only half the picture. For all their strengths there are corresponding weaknesses. The single biggest weakness on their part is their refusal to understand our culture and society. The United States of America is a difficult place to understand for someone who is not originally from here. I was born here, and I do not claim to fully comprehend all that goes on around me. For a foreign terrorist group, especially one from a traditional Islamic culture, that lack of understanding is much deeper. The society that these people come from is far simpler and has much less depth than ours. We are a multi-cultural society and theirs is not. In their world, things have been more or less the same for centuries; nothing changes in any large way as the generations pass. Everything has its place and that set of circumstances is relied upon by all. America, on the other hand, seems to change almost daily.

A terrorist group that is not from here will have a difficult time operating unless they have the help of people who have been here long enough to be assimilated into our culture. The hardcore members of the organization may not fully trust these second generation people, yet they will have no choice about enlisting second generational aid. Absent such help, the terrorist group risks exposure-that exposure could mean their destruction. Of all the weaknesses inherent to an Islamic terror organization, one stands above all others.

The members of any such group are primarily male and carry the attitudes and outlooks of the culture that they came from. Their world is a controlled world, that fact will manifest itself in many ways. Nowhere will this regulation be more evident than in the relationship between the sexes. Islamic societies, in their purer forms, take the normal relationship between men and women and turn it into one of hatred and mistrust. Young men are taught that the female of the species represents an inherent threat to their religious virtue. They are taught that any contact outside of marriage is by its very nature, sinful and destructive. In many of those cultures, men and women are denied any normal relationship. This indoctrination cannot conquer the mechanics of biology, however, and even while they are taught to feel hatred and contempt for the fairer sex, they experience the normal feelings of male sexual desire. In their societies, there is usually no easy outlet for this desire so they simply suffer in silence or find other ways of satisfying this basic human need. If they find themselves in our society, however, things change.

The prevalence of sexual imagery in our culture can be overpowering. Actual sexual contact is probably not as frequent as what is suggested, but we are inundated with visual imagery. This is not all that distracting for us, as we have simply become accustomed to it. The subject gets mentioned now and again during religious and cultural debates but that is about as far as it goes. Men like to look at naked or near naked women, and the advertisement industry has tuned to the fact that this tendency can be used to sell just about anything. Contact between male and female, sexual or otherwise, is an expected part of our lives and does not represent any oddity for the majority of our citizens. For the terrorist operative, coming from a restrictive Islamic society, the visual buffet offered by our culture can be overwhelming.

The Islamic terrorist, operating on our soil will be immediately drawn to the vices of our society, primarily alcohol and sex. He will be so fixated on these delights that he may allow his pursuit of them to interfere with his ability to carry out a mission. He can be as religiously dedicated as he wants and he is still prone to these temptations. I would go as far as to say that maybe the more devout he claims to be, the more susceptible he is. In my eleven plus years with the U.S. State Department Anti-terrorist Assistance Program, I have had the opportunity to instruct people from all over the Islamic world. Upon reaching our shores, one of the first things that they all proclaim is the dedication that they have to the principles and teachings of Islam. Prior to their arrival in Louisiana, this may have been true. However, once they are here for a few weeks that outlook tends to change. Baton Rouge can provide the weary traveler with anything that is available elsewhere and this accommodation includes the vices of alcohol and sex. Strip clubs and bars dot the bayou landscape and some are an easy distance to where these foreign students stay. Within a few weeks, they can usually be found laying siege to the bar in one of these establishments. Their religious dedication is long forgotten in the face of the visual paradise laid before them. Happily, they set about trying to drink the place dry, while determining just how many dollar bills will actually fit in a few inches of g-string.

This attraction to the seamier side of western culture can also manifest itself closer to their homeland. There is a phenomenon in the Arab world that is not widely known to most westerners. This is simply the cultural concept of being "out from under the eyes of Allah." If he is not currently being watched by the Almighty, a person from that region may feel that they can do pretty much whatever they want. After all if God cannot see you, he is not as likely to get irritated as you wallow in sin. This situation is demonstrated physically as well as verbally. On any commercial flight going into Saudi Arabia, there will be a terse announcement in Arabic when the aircraft reaches the point to where it is fifty or so miles outside of Saudi airspace. The effect of this announcement on the passengers is electrifying. Cigarettes are crushed out, drinks are rapidly finished, and whole packs of breath mints are crunched. The women frantically set about sewing themselves into one of those head to toe black bags that are all the rage in that society. These folks enter into this frenzy of activity because the pilot has been so kind as to warn them that God will be able to see them soon, so they had better start acting like it. On a commercial flight out of Saudi Arabia, the opposite activity takes place. At the fifty mile mark the pilot will come on the intercom and in a relaxed tone will inform them that they have given the Heavenly Father the visual slip and it's party time. Ties are loosened, the black bags come off, and the drink cart makes its first of many trips down the aisle. If you confront one of these individuals about the subject, they will be initially evasive. If pressed, however, they will eventually admit that their activities have less to do with God seeing them than the religious police who control daily life in their nation. They fully realize that the visual range of the Creator includes the European and North American continent. They are not stupid people and they know that, when it comes to God, they are fooling nobody, least of all him.

So, how do they account for this duplicity? Well, for the most part, they don't. They do not necessarily see the situation the same way that we do. Most of these people have no concept of hypocrisy as we know it in western culture. There is no idea of "practice what you preach" to guide daily life. Their outlook allows them to ignore the teachings of their religion if it is convenient to the moment. Make no mistake, this temporary setting aside of the tenants and rules of their religion in no way reduces their devotion to that religion. So, how can this contradiction be? Well, again, the answer is that there is no actual contradiction in their minds, because they don't think like we do. Their way of looking at the world may be inexplicable to us, but we should understand that is their way. These people can come and live in our societies for decades, availing themselves of every benefit inherent to our culture, including moving and working among us and smile the whole time. Yet, at any given moment, they have the capacity to enter into a plot to destroy us. Some of the more radical ones can drink their way across the United States, daily violating one of the basic laws of their religion, and still have the nerve to sit in the cockpit of a jet airliner and fly it into a building at five hundred miles per hour. Friends, stop and think for a moment about the level of sheer nerve that action must have required. What is inconceivable to us is natural to them. Personally, I have concluded that their outlook is both strength and a weakness. It is strength because it allows them the ability to carry out a mission regardless of their current level of sin. It is a weakness because their attraction to that sin can distract them from their mission.

Of all their deficiencies, it is their inherent lack of ability to control their emotions that is the greatest threat to them. In western culture we are taught from childhood to control our emotions and feelings. Obviously, not every single citizen of this society gets this message but in comparison to those from the Islamic world, we are paragons of self control. How many times have you turned on your television set and seen them howling and screaming en masse over something or other? The cause of the insanity may be the death of a leader or a perceived insult to their religion. On the other hand, there may be no particular cause to the event, it was just time to shout and scream. They are slaves to their emotions and are, for the most part, incapable of controlling those feelings. As a result, they are some of the most easily manipulated people on the planet. Present them with a certain set of circumstances, and their reaction is entirely predictable. The situation in Iraq is a prime example. The presence of U.S. military forces in that nation serves as such a magnet to the Jihadists that everybody with an AK-47 and attitude heads for Baghdad to kill Americans. This has served to bog them down in that conflict to the same level as us. So fixated are they on this issue that they have completely neglected to attack us at home. Let's hope that trend continues.

As with the previous chapter many more words can be written on this subject. On the other hand, I am again convinced that I have provided you with much more real information than the national news media ever will. I encourage you to dig further. Ignorance may be bliss in some circumstances, but this is not one of those circumstances. In this war, ignorance is a potential path to the graveyard.

Chapter 4

The America Haters

"Woe unto them that call evil good and good evil."

Bible: Isaiah 5:20

So far the discussion in this book has focused on the terrorists themselves. However, they are not the total picture. There are others involved in this struggle as well. They have the ability to do as much harm as the Jihadists, if not more. I refer to these folks as "the America haters," because that is exactly what they are. They come in all shapes and sizes, both of a foreign nature and a domestic one. I have listened to them all of my life, and you probably have as well. Every night they squawk at us from the television set and their ramblings adorn the morning news pages. The message is always the same, "Everything is America's fault." If there is a problem on this planet, these folks will find a way to blame it on the United States. Even if there is obviously no connection between the United States and the said problem, they will find a way to twist it so that the blame lands on us. For decades we have been subjected to a never-ending stream of this garbage, and it seems to come from all sides. If you were to believe everything that you hear and read, you would probably come to the conclusion that America is the most hated nation in human history.

It gets tiresome, I know, but irritating as these people are, they will always be here. They are one of the prices that must be paid to live in a free society. That being said, it is important to understand who they are and why they do the things that they do.

The Europeans

"One should look long and carefully at one's self before one considers judging others."

Moliere

French playwright 1600's

Of all the America haters, the Europeans are the ones I understand the least. Our present stands on their past, and as I look at them today, I can only ask "Neighbors, what on earth happened to you?" All of the freedoms that we enjoy in modern America originated from their continent. Long before the Boston Tea Party or the battles of Lexington and Concord, the idea of human liberty struggled to be born in Europe. Even before the French dismantled their own royal bonds, they helped us get rid of ours. The very concept of liberty and freedom for the individual was born in the post-Renaissance European continent. So what happened to make them such sniveling cowards in modern times? What occurred in their societies to make them abandon the precious ideas that they helped to create?

Well, the truth is simple but disturbing. The primary factor behind the flight of European societies from the ideals of western culture has been a large-scale rejection of the Christian religion. Rather than being proud of this heritage and its accomplishments, Europeans have wallowed in decades of anti-religious propaganda. As they struggle to become more secular and sophisticated, they lean from the concept of individual liberty and more toward socialism with all its inherent lack of concern for individual liberty. In a desire to move from the constrictions of a religious code, they move toward an ideology whose main tenet is restriction of individual freedom. Ironically, at the same time that they are fleeing their own religion they have made themselves vulnerable to the religion of hostile foreigners, i.e. Islamic radicals.

Christianity has had its bad times as has every other religion. Yet it has also bestowed some gifts to the world that we have today. The basic concept of individual liberty was founded in Christianity.

Therefore, to reject ones religious heritage is to reject the benefits of that heritage. The citizens of the European continent have rejected their religious origins because life has become easy and the focus of their society has turned to other things. Having fun and partying is the primary goal of most of their citizens and Christianity tends to get in the way of that. Christian religion is hated because it instructs that some activities are right and some are wrong. It informs all that there are consequences to certain actions and some of these consequences are extreme. As societies become more and more comfortable, and life gets easier, the less people want to hear this message.

That's where the hatred comes from, and this resentment is the basis for the Europeans dislike of America. A large portion of Americans maintain a societal sense of morality and make no apology for it. We have a cultural sense of religion and work to pass this concept on to our children. They consider this to be backward and un-sophisticated. Unfortunately for them, at the same time that they seek to flee the constraints of religion they have opened up their borders to a flood of foreign immigrants whose entire lives are ruled by religion. So here they all sit, secular societies focused on partying and phony sophistication, infiltrated by people who are largely focused on God. How they ever thought that this cohabitation would work is beyond me. As Islamic mobs rampage though their cities burning and destroying, modern Europeans stand bewildered and question how such things could have come to pass. Gee, I wonder.

Like many Americans, the Europeans have confused the concepts of liberty and license. They pay lip service to the concept of liberty but, license to wallow consequence free in debauchery is what they really want. History has taught us that liberty is a double-edged sword. Along with freedom, it carries with it a tremendous amount of personal responsibility. License, on the other hand, is much more fun and only requires basic human desires to accomplish. In their pursuit of insignificant pleasure and leisure, and in the abandonment of the Christian religion, the Europeans are digging their own "cultural grave." If things over there keep going the way they are, that grave is going to be filled real soon.

The Locals

"A fool can always find a greater fool to admire him."

Nicolas Boileau

French poet

The domestic America haters fall into several different groups. Some hate this country for political reasons, and some for social reasons. Whatever their viewpoint, they would see this country, as we know it, destroyed and something else put in its place. What exactly that something else is depends on who is doing the hating, but you can be assured of one fact. Whatever world these folks want to create is not one in which you would want to live.

The Entertainment Industry

"A dreary industrial town controlled by hoodlums of enormous wealth, the ethical sense of a pack of jackals, and taste so degraded that it befouled everything."

S. J. Perelman

American screenwriter and author, talking about Hollywood

The movie and television industry is chock full of America haters. They would vociferously deny this fact, but it is the truth. Many in this industry seek to denigrate and destroy the society around them. Given a choice, they will automatically align themselves in opposition to our cultural norms. The amount of movies produced over the last few decades, denigrating America, far outnumbers the amount of movies praising it. Even if America and its culture is not the main subject of the film or television show, they will usually find a way to throw rocks at it. Certainly these people have a right to do what they are doing and I would make

51

no attempt to interfere with their activities even if it were in my power to do so. Nor would I stand idly by as others try to silence them. Their speech, and a movie is certainly a form of speech, is constitutionally protected. That does not mean, however, that they should be immune from criticism of that speech. Sometimes I think that the liberal community forgets that all of the rest of us have a right to speak, and are as free to criticize them as they are to criticize us. If you listen to them squawk the few times when verbal criticism is leveled at their industry, you would think that they are being rounded up and sent to the gulag. These persons equate disagreement with censorship and I take issue with that view. Boys and girls of the entertainment world, if you put an idea out there for public consumption then you have to be prepared for the possibility that not everyone will like the taste.

Other than incessant America bashing, the issue I have with many of those in the entertainment industry is their overwhelming hypocrisy. They hate this country, all the while benefiting from its existence. They support every socialist cause and champion this ideology every chance that they get, while practicing pure, cut-throat, free market capitalism. They talk about the evils of the rich and the need for massive redistribution of wealth, while sitting on mounds of money that they hire platoons of accountants to protect. They moan about world poverty and the inequities of life on planet earth, all the while living a lifestyle that is unreachable by most human beings. They weep at me from my television screen as they wander through some third world garbage dump, imploring me to be more generous with my money and then return to the mansion worth more than all of the people that they supposedly champion will earn in their collective lifetimes. They support any politician who proposes to raise taxes while hiding behind high paid accounting firms that will guarantee that they never feel the fiscal reality of the idea that they support.

Even worse, many of them assume expertise on any subject that they have portrayed on the screen. More than one of them have testified in front of congress on select issues without the least qualification to do so. Years ago, the actress Meryl Strep spent a session in front of the House of Representatives talking about the problem of a harmful chemical in the nation's apple crop. She felt entitled to do this simply because she had played the role of an apple farmer's wife in some silly movie. She never actually performed the job for real, just played the part and therefore deemed herself certified to lecture the rest of us about it. I wish this story ended with mere apples but, unfortunately, it doesn't.

No other group in our society, with the possible exception of the media, considers itself more qualified to tell the rest of us how to live our lives. There is no evidence of this qualification; in fact, the only evidence is to the contrary. I can think of no group less fit to advise the rest of us on life than those in the entertainment industry. Their whole profession is built on the concept of pretending to be something that they are not. Nevertheless, the lectures continue. The majority of them cannot keep a marriage together for more than a few months. Yet, they unhesitatingly harangue us on the realities of that institution. Some of them change sexual partners like well-trained infantrymen change socks. In another direction, most of them have never served a day in uniform and would shudder at the thought of actual military service but because they played a part in some war movie they feel equipped to tell us about the realities of warfare. Well, having spent a lifetime as a soldier, I can tell them that the reality is this: going through some week long Hollywood whiners' boot camp isn't even close to the real thing and does not qualify you as an information source on anything even remotely connected to the military.

Most of these folks live in a totally phony world and can offer us nothing of any value when it comes to life's real questions. Fortunately, there may be a simple answer to this predicament. Maybe they should just stick to entertainment and leave the rest of it alone. Realistically, I would not suggest that you hold your breath waiting for that to happen. If you do, you may experience some physiological difficulties.

The Media

"The cruelest lies are often told in silence."

Robert Lewis Stevenson

British writer

The modern American news media has become the single most culturally destructive institution in human history. For years they have indoctrinated the citizens of this nation into ignorance and cowardice. The harm that has been done by this institution has been enormous and we may never know the true cost. As America haters they have no equal, and they do not always try to hide this fact. I have watched them my entire life and I know their techniques and methods like the back of my hand. Folks, anyone who claims that these people are not anti-American is either deaf or doesn't listen to them. They will lose no opportunity to denigrate this nation and undermine any attempt on its part to protect itself or its interests. They never met a foreign America hater that they did not like. They had a love affair with every communist dictator of the past and present and supported this ideology throughout the entire cold war. In fact many of them are still romantically attached. Just the other morning, I turned on my television in time to witness Diane Sawyer, recently retuned from a trip to North Korea, practically swooning as she described how well bathed and clean she had found the subjects of the slave state. To hear her babble, you would have thought she had just come from an earthly paradise. On the other hand, I did not get the impression that she was ready to trade in her trendy Manhattan pad for a change of citizenship.

In the present conflict, the dominant media has acted no different. Oh, they conjured up a few weeks of luke warm patriotism in the aftermath of 9/11, but that is well past. In this conflict, as in others, they seek to make excuses for the actions of our enemies, while heaping criticism on our own activities. They focus on any failure on the part of America and routinely ignore all of our successes. In the event that we are facing any military conflict, the enemy forces will be presented to the American public as the greatest soldiers since the Roman Legion, while our own military will be subjected to doubt and ridicule. When we win the encounter, our success will be discounted as some fluke of just dumb luck. Their coverage of the situation in Iraq is a prime example of what I am talking about. When was the last time you turned on the news and listened to anything good from the media on this subject? When have you seen a pro American Iraqi interviewed about anything? For that matter, when have you seen a pro American anybody interviewed about any subject? The fact is that you probably have not, and that is no accident.

On the domestic front, many news media activities follow the same pattern. They will continually seek out the bad side to any issue, especially if it casts our traditional society and its traditional values in a bad light. Nowhere is this ingrained bias more evident than when it comes to religious beliefs, especially Christianity. The contempt and derision that most of these people feel for those who live their lives by any sort of religious code is physically evident in their discussion of the issue. Even when they manage to keep the smirk off their face, it comes through in the tone of their voice. On the other hand, anyone who lives a life in opposition to a religious moral code is accorded immediate hero status and rubbed in the American public's face at every opportunity. The weirder the better, it seems, and every time I think they have found the biggest freak on the planet, they come up with one that is even worse. During the interviews of such strange creatures, the interviewing reporter is awestruck just to be in the near holy presence of some babbling idiot with green hair, Satan tattoos, and a bone through their nose (Dennis Rodman is a good example.) I think that some of them are so hero struck that if the freak decided to tell them to jump out of the window the next thing that we would see is their rapidly disappearing posterior as it headed downward to street level. If the weirdo in question offers any opinion hostile to conventional American values (especially traditional Christian values) then the interviewer will come close to fainting out of sheer adulation. At the same time it is interesting to witness their outright cowardice when it comes to confronting the radical side of Islam: A far more combative and intolerant religion than modern Christianity. Zealous as they are when it comes to beating up on people of faith, they don't appear to want to confront the religion of Muhammad, do they?

The bulk of our news media does not wish to see any success in our efforts to defend ourselves or our interests. Many of the people in this profession were college educated in the 60's and 70's. During that process, they were indoctrinated into a "blame America first" mentality. They believe it is their duty to maintain an adversarial relationship with this nation in order to keep things straight or act as some sort of watchdog over this society. When asked about who watches over them and keeps them straight, they generally have no reply and seem puzzled by the question. Over the last few years there has been a slow change for the better in this area (Fox News), but the overwhelming majority of the people in this profession are still hostile to this nation and all for which it stands.

The Conspiracy Theories

"Everyone is entitled to his own opinion. He is not entitled to his own facts."

Daniel Patrick Moynihand

U.S. Senator, State of New York

Unfortunately, the conspiracy theorists are a group that I know quite a bit about as I grew up around this belief. According to these folks, everything that happens on planet earth can be attributed to a small group of plotters who lurk about conspiring to relieve you of your liberty and in some cases, your life. In the main scenario, the U.S. Government has been totally infiltrated by hostile foreigners who are busy bringing about a never ending era of socialist dictatorship. Backed up with the power and force of the United Nations (an ineffective institution if there ever was one), these people are responsible for every bad event that has happened on this planet. The power and ability of these folks is incredible. According to some theories, they control Mother Nature and cause massive calamities like the Indonesian tidal wave. There are folks out there who believe that the 2002 tsunami was brought about by the C.I.A. and they caused the tidal wave by using some sort of super sized cell phone up in Alaska. Other conspiracy theorists would have you accept that it was the federal government that carried out the 9/11 attacks and the Oklahoma City bombing years before. Why they did this is not clearly explained by the conspiracy crowd, but it has something to do with further erosion of our liberties. They have not yet gotten around to blaming the Gulf Coast hurricanes of 2005 on this source but, be patient, they will.

Some of these theories sound kind of plausible when they are first presented. They are set up to prey on people's natural frustration with governmental inefficiency and incompetence. These are feelings that we have all had at one time or another. However, when the conspiracy theorists are asked logical questions they seem to get confused and hostile. The promoters of these view points will be some of the friendliest folks that you will ever meet, right up to the time that you question their views. Then you will unwittingly become a charter member of the Bush/Halliburton/ Zionist/CIA/New World Order/Masonic/Illuminate/United Nations/ black-helicopter/blow up the New Orleans levy/we didn't land on the moon, conspiracy for global domination. At that point, they will become some of the unfriendliest folks that you have ever met.

The lazy way of thinking

"This is exactly they type of 'journalism' one would expect to find in a dictatorship like that of Saddam Hussein's Iraq."

Debunking 9/11 Myths

Published by: Popular Mechanics Magazine

To believe in conspiracies, especially all-powerful global ones, is an intellectually lazy way of viewing the world. This thought process results in an abandonment of societal responsibility. For the dedicated conspiracy buff, all the normal problems of life can now be blamed on a shadowy, all-powerful group of plotters. Personal shortcomings can now be explained as the fault of others. There is no reason to believe in anything or work toward a better world. There is not even a responsibility to participate in any voting process, local or national, because the ongoing conspiracy invalidates the results. Everything is pre-ordained to failure and nothing can be done to change it. The holders of these beliefs are free to endlessly criticize everything around them and are not obligated to lift a finger in the betterment of the place that they live. What a deal!

I don't believe in the conspiracies, folks. They make no sense and most of them are outside the realm of human ability to bring about. That doesn't mean that there are no problems out there. There are people in positions of power in this nation that do not have the respect and reverence for the Constitution that they should have. There people in all levels of government who seek to gain more and more power over the citizens that they serve. All around are people in positions of authority that think only of their own gain and care nothing for the responsibilities of their position. These people are in our society and have been in every society created by humans. That doesn't mean that the conspiracy theories are true.

In the twisted mind of the conspiracy theorists you have few choices available to you. You can whole heartedly agree with their views, no matter how far fetched. You can hold this position only as long as you accept everything they say without question or doubt. The moment that you dare to disagree you will be placed on trial. The procedure will only last a few seconds, but in that small space of time you will be convicted and sentenced. You will be afforded no opportunity to speak on your own behalf and nothing positive about you or your life will be taken into account. Your character, patriotism, courage, and lifetime of dedication to principles or ideals will be ignored. Neither your personal experience nor your knowledge will be admitted into the proceedings. Upon sentencing, you will be placed in one of two categories.

The first category will be that you are a member of the conspiracy and you will be deemed to have betrayed everything that you believe in (including your own family.) From that point forward, every action on your part will be viewed from this angle. One of the most disturbing things about these people is their ability to accuse fellow citizens, friends, and relatives of complicity with pure evil. They do so without hesitation or remorse. This is a window onto the true content of their character, and the view is not a pretty one.

The other category that the conspiracy theorist will place you in is that you are so stupid and uncomprehending of the world around you that you have been duped into participating in the plot. Once you have been placed into this category, you will be viewed with pity and scorn. The conspiracy theorist will look at you in much the same manner as they would a mentally impaired child. Again, you will have no defense available to you. Anything you say, regardless of your experience or background, will be dismissed because you are obviously not capable of recognizing the truth.

Of the two categories I don't know which one is worse. Neither one is deserved or fair. Of all of the "America haters" out there, the conspiracy theorists are the ones that I hold in the most contempt.

They will always be with us.

I know that listening to America haters makes you angry and I certainly share that sentiment. It is hard to watch and listen while people castigate this nation, at the same time enjoying its many benefits. Benefits purchased with the blood and suffering of people far stronger and braver than they will ever be. Be that as it may, the America haters have always been here and they probably always will be. In every civilization throughout human history, there have been those who tried to undermine and destroy the very culture that sustained their existence. There is nothing that can be done about these individuals directly and I would not stand by and see their basic rights violated. As long as they stay within the bounds of the law, I would do nothing to prevent them from offering their opinions and influence to others. If I had all of the power on earth I would neither say nor do anything to stop the activities of the Michael Moores, the Cindy Sheehans or the Genene Grenafalos. I would do nothing to the Jesse Jacksons or the Al Sharptons. Even if

I had the power to make them shut up, I would not use that power to keep them from speaking freely. Believe me; I would be far more respectful of their rights in this situation than they would be of mine. Folks like these are simply part of the price that has to be paid in order to have a free society. The biggest mistake that can be made is granting them too much attention when they put their hypocrisy and insanity on display. They have a right to speak. We have no obligation to listen.

Another way to counter these people is to verbally challenge them at every opportunity. For the last three decades they have run their mouth with little to no opposition. For the most part, they controlled the media and the entertainment industry. Very few voices were raised in protest and those that were, seemed small and weak compared to the opposition that they faced. Fortunately, times tend to change. With the invention of the internet and other forms of communication technology, total control has been wrested from these people. Their voice is no longer the only one to be heard, and that is driving them nuts. So be angry if you must, but be angry in a smart way.

These folks fear a calm, competent challenge, especially in the public arena. Despite all the lip service that they pay to the idea of free speech, most America haters would prefer to reserve that particular commodity for themselves. Therefore, when you see an opportunity, challenge them and challenge them hard. Don't worry about fairness or balance, the simple fact that you challenged them is balance. Find any weakness that you can and turn that weakness against them. You are not trying to convince them that you are right and they are wrong. One of our problems has always been that we think if we just present logic, then these folks will see things our way. That is an exercise in futility for the simple reason that they don't see the issues like we do, and their motivations are different. What we should concentrate on is defeating them and that means reducing their cultural and political influence in this society. If we can achieve that, even on a small scale, then we will have accomplished far more than if we try to win them over. When the opportunity arises, challenge and defeat them. When they cease to argue and start to call you vile names, you will know that you are on the right track.

Those of us on the conservative side of the fence tend to think and act more individualistically and independently than those on the America hating left. We do not routinely band together and raise our voices in communal speech. For that reason, we have a tendency to think that we fight alone. This can lead to a sense of isolation and frustration. This perception has led to many of us being far too ready to concede defeat, especially on social issues. We need to realize that we are not alone and never have been. Recent political history shows us that our side is actually more powerful than theirs in many ways. In 1994, a small, relatively uncoordinated, conservative political movement resulted in the leftists losing forty plus years of accumulated power in the U.S. Senate and House of Representatives. They have been trying to recover from that traumatic event for the last twelve years with little success. Even their gains in 2006 brought them only a fraction of the power that they once had. They can just as easily lose that a couple of years down the road. Cultural changes in the aftermath of 9/11 have hit them even harder, and their ideology and influence is at the lowest point that I have seen in my lifetime. That being said, they are still a force to be reckoned with and here is why.

The main strategic difference between the two sides is that anything short of a total defeat, they view as a victory, and anything short of total victory we view as a defeat. Our side has a habit of psychologically giving in before the fight is over and sometimes before it even starts. During the course of my life, I have heard far more defeatist talk from my side than theirs. This has to stop. The America haters operate on a distinctly incremental mindset. They would love to achieve a sweeping success, but they know that it is not likely to happen. What they do is move their agenda ahead any way they can, no matter how small or seemingly insignificant the issue. Most of the time, small successes are all that they achieve. However, when you add up all those small steps, they turn into major gains. This is how they accumulated so much power despite being numerically inferior. We need to adopt some of the same strategy and stop trying to win everything in one battle. If we can learn this lesson, then their days of major influence are over and victory in the cultural war will be ours. There is an old saying that maintains that things are never over until they are actually over. Those who love America and embrace its cultural and moral values, are not in the minority and never have been. We need to realize this and act accordingly. So, keep the faith, my friends, especially on the dark days. More belief and optimism on our side will be bad news for theirs.

Chapter 5

The Role of the Military

"I do solemnly swear that I will support and defend the Constitution of the United States against all enemies, foreign and domestic."

Oath of Enlistment

Armed Forces of the United States

Until a few years ago, it would have been easy for an uninitiated outsider to get the wrong idea of why our military services existed. If one did not know better, one could have quickly come to the conclusion that the sole function of these institutions was to ensure that every single American youth had the opportunity to go to college on the taxpayer's dime. A more understandable deduction would have been that the primary purpose of these organizations was to serve as giant test beds for liberal experiments in social engineering. There have been some improvements in this perception since 9/11, but confusion is still in evidence in a large part of our population.

It would be tempting to let the blame for these misunderstandings lay with influences outside the military, and some of it does. The truth, however, requires us to also look at the institutions themselves. For decades the military establishment in this country sought to camouflage its real purpose for being here and, in its advertising, displayed itself as everything other than what it is. The military has spent hundreds of millions of dollars telling the youth of America that they can be part of an organization, one which only exists for the purpose of violent conflict, and somehow be guaranteed to never participate in such an endeavor.

For decades, the U.S. Army (one of the worst offenders) has focused its recruiting advertisements on everything but ground combat, the only function of the organization. In a series of deliberately misleading messages, smiling youths are portrayed doing everything except killing enemy personnel and being killed in return. All sorts of catchy slogans have been introduced in an attempt to disguise the very nature of military service and the risks that it entails. This dishonesty has served to indoctrinate the American masses into believing that their military institutions are nothing more than a series of gigantic trade schools. Originally, this was done so that the organizations could try to separate themselves from the legacy of the Vietnam conflict, but the trend has continued, and honesty has always been in short supply. Nowhere has this institutional deceitfulness been more evident than in the recruiting of reserves and National Guard personnel. This aspect of military service has been long sold as an alternative to the nastier side of active duty; kind of like sticking your toe in the water but never having to get completely wet. When the 1990/1991Gulf War occurred, that myth was shattered as thousands of reserves and guard personnel found themselves on the way to a real war. In the months that followed, the American public was treated to a lot of whining and complaining on the part of some of these individuals. As a professional soldier, I have no sympathy! It was his or her own fault. Any quick look at history would have shown them the fallacy of their belief. Both the First and Second World War were fought with the help of hundreds of thousands of reserves and guardsmen. Thousands more were deployed to Korea and Vietnam. Thousands more have been deployed to Afghanistan and Iraq. Even more will be deployed to future conflicts.

In the pre-Vietnam era, military service was looked upon far more realistically that it has been since that conflict. People who joined up in those days did not carry the false illusions that plague many of their modern day counterparts. Those who signed up or were drafted during the World Wars knew full well the nature of the organizations that they were joining and, if they did not, the institutions quickly set them straight. Those folks knew that they were there for the purpose of violent conflict and accepted that as fact. They may not have been happy about the truth, but they recognized the truth and most of them adopted the "lets get it done" attitude and set about business. Many of these people did not necessarily enjoy military service (it has its rough side, believe me) and would not have chosen it as an occupation; never-the-less these citizens did the job and carried away a well deserved pride in having served their country. There was a far more developed sense of patriotism and duty in those days and only recently have there been some improvements in this area.

The Vietnam legacy

"Who controls the past controls the future: who controls the present controls the past."

George Orwell

British author and journalist

The majority of the problems suffered by our military came about in the latter years of the Vietnam War and its aftermath. In that conflict this nation sent people into harms way with little or no desire to see the event through to an acceptable end. At the highest levels of our government, there seemed to be nothing but apathy and confusion about why we were there and what is was we hoped to accomplish. The war drug on and on, the casualties mounted, and the end was nowhere in sight. It is little wonder that things eventually fell apart. As the situation worsened, it played right into the hands of our domestic enemies and they used it to full advantage. Arguments about the war and other social issues were used to tear this nation apart and we are still feeling the effects today. The result was a humiliating retreat and the destructive aftermath of the decision to withdraw. The legacy of this time is one of the primary reasons that we are so hesitant to defend our interests and ourselves in present times.

In the years following Vietnam, the armed forces of this nation were in pretty sad shape. I enlisted during this time period and things were pretty grim. Morale was at rock bottom; the training was unrealistic at best and dangerously inadequate at worst. Equipment was in disrepair or never worked right to begin with. There was an apathetic, self-denial aspect to much of military life. War was something that theoretically could happen but no one (individuals and individual units aside) took it seriously. Drug abuse was rampant; racial animosity permeated the organizations, and the discipline and training necessary to prevail in any sort of conflict did not exist. This sorry state of affairs hit rock bottom with the aborted Iran rescue operation in 1980. Humiliated in front of the entire world, the American people decided it was time for a change.

The long road back

"Of the four wars in my lifetime, none came about because the U.S. was too strong".

Ronald Reagan

40th President of the United States

The election of Ronald Reagan signaled the beginning of a new era for our armed forces. We now had a president whose primary occupation was not apologizing for this nation's existence. This man understood the inherent goodness of this society, and he was determined for our ideology to triumph over that of our communist opponents. Within months of his inauguration, a feeling of renewal began to sweep through the military and things began to change. The first order of business was the reestablishment of discipline. Without discipline, a military organization is just a uniformed mob. Next order of business was the drug problem. Offenders began to find themselves weeded from the ranks. New equipment and training was placed into operation, along with the arrival of new organizations and enhanced capabilities. Our mission began to be more clearly defined; to defend the United States and its interests around the globe. President Reagan had decided that defeating our foes could best protect our interest and security and we set about building up to do just that. This man was one of the few human beings in a position of power to have the courage to call evil, *evil.* He applied this label to the Soviet Union, much to the horror of our domestic enemies. America haters hated this man like no other president before him or after.

With this era came the first shooting conflicts since Vietnam. These operations did not come off all that well. It had been decades since our forces had seen action and there was a lot of rust. The occupation of the Beirut airport in 1982-1983 ended in disaster. A small contingent of U.S. Marines were dispatched to secure the international airport and attempt some sort of peacekeeping process. This operation was ill prepared, and it was obvious from the start that almost no thought process had been put into the mission. It was simply a knee jerk reaction to the spreading violence in the region and an attempt to exert U.S. influence over the situation. This endeavor was doomed to failure from the start and only served to place young Americans into a deadly scenario. The unwillingness of both the U.S. government and the military to see the reality of the situation was evident in the news footage of Marines patrolling this war-torn city with empty weapons. It was a disaster waiting to happen and the horror show was not long in coming. In 1983, attacks against American forces in the city began to increase and we found ourselves drawn deeper into the conflict. Casualties began to rise and the American public began to lose their initial, half-hearted, support for the operation. As the confrontation turned more and more vicious, the desire to bug-out became all prevailing back home.

In October of 1983, Islamic terrorists conducted a massive suicide bombing of the Beirut Airport administration building. This structure was being used as a large barracks to house hundreds of Marines. This situation was a clear violation of one of the basic rules of ground combat, which is never to bunch together. The result of the terrorist attack left 180 plus Marines dead and hundreds wounded. Television news carried the pictures of the carnage worldwide and the lack of U.S. preparation and resolve was on display for all to see. One of the small facts that came out in the aftermath of the incident was that the Marine sentries on duty at the front gate of the building were incapable of stopping the attacking vehicle because they were carrying unloaded weapons. The fact that Marines were *still carrying unloaded weapons after the attack,* goes to show how far the American military had deviated from the mind-set necessary for success in combat. Clearly, we still had a long way to go.

A mere two days after the Beirut bombing, the United States conducted the invasion of the small Caribbean island nation of Grenada. Although this operation was a tactical success, it was plagued with problems and almost failed several times. No blame can be attached to the dedication and bravery of the Marines and Soldiers involved but should be assigned to the mind-set of the military as a whole. It was obvious during this operation that the military had been doing little thinking about war and was learning the process all over again. It had been a long time since Vietnam and the edge was gone. The American public watched the operation with trepidation, ready to shy away from the conflict and demand withdraw. Fortunately, it was over before it could go too badly and give us an excuse to run away.

In 1989 the U.S. invasion of Panama was launched. This operation developed fairly well. Many of the bitter lessons learned in the Grenada operation were put into effect with success as the result. The Panamanian defense forces were willing to fight in some cases but were quickly overwhelmed and scattered by U.S. firepower. The specter of post-invasion guerilla warfare conducted by Noriega holdouts never materialized, so we walked away from that one relatively unscathed. Had the situation dragged on, it might have been a different story.

Late in 1990 came the Kuwait situation. Saddam Hussein's invasion of his tiny neighbor set the stage for the largest American military operation since the Second World War. Although President Bush organized a coalition of over a hundred nations, the bulk of the military force was going to have to come from the United States and everybody knew it. We were the only nation with the military might necessary for any such venture and we were going to have to carry most of the load. United States military personnel were going to have to go halfway around the world and confront an enemy that had the ability to absorb and produce thousands of casualties. The military was going to have its resolve and courage tested. American citizens were going to have their own will examined in the process.

This was no small-time operation in our back yard; this was a direct confrontation halfway around the world. The enemy had the numbers to match ours and was believed to have the expertise as well. As it turned out, they did not have such a capability, but there was no way to know that beforehand. It was obvious from the start that the U.S. military had made vast improvements and appeared to be up to the game. This appearance was proven as fact in the next several months as the forces of Sadam Hussein were bombed into oblivion and crushed by a massive ground assault. The war on the ground was over in less that a week and the casualties were extremely light. The American public was overjoyed at the short duration of the conflict and the ease of victory. Now don't get me wrong here folks; I was as overjoyed as anyone else at the quick victory and would not have wished things to be any other way. On the other hand, military professionals like myself would look at this conflict and worry that it had set a precedent in the mind of the American public. If it did, that precedent might prove impossible to reproduce in any future conflicts. As it turned out, Operation Desert Storm taught the American citizens several erroneous lessons and these lessons were retained into the next decade.

When the ground assault finally came, it was conducted under a news blackout imposed by the military. The military had their reasons; considering the destructive and treasonous actions of the American media in the Vietnam War, I don't blame the military for opting the press out. The down-side of this decision was that the American public ultimately viewed a sanitized version of the events. For the most part there were no pictures of casualties, and it seemed to be a bloodless conflict for our side. Of course, the Iraqis didn't fare so well and that aspect was displayed for all to see. The reality was that there were also U.S. casualties in the ground war and some of the fighting was vicious. Men and vehicles were lost to enemy actions and body bags were filled, but the American public was spared this vision. As a result many Americans came to the conclusion that ground confrontations could be conducted without significant casualties. The first Iraq War led the average citizen to believe that wars could be fought with airpower alone, and that laser guided bombs could be used to solve any problem. In two short years they were to learn differently.

The media focused on the laser-guided bomb aspect of the conflict for the simple reason that it made for sensational television clips. In a society becoming obsessed with video games, the pictures coming on the television screen of munitions flying through windows was exciting and captivating. In general, the media would not discuss the fact that these precision weapons only represented a small fraction of the aerial munitions used. The majority of the bombs dropped in this conflict were of the old unguided variety and many of them missed their targets. At the end of weeks of aerial attacks, the Iraqi Army was relatively intact and appeared willing to fight. It was the ground element which had to enter the battle and settle the matter, just as these soldiers have in all of our other conflicts.

Our will falters again

The U.S. intervention in Somalia in 1992 initially took on the aspect of a gigantic media circus as the press corps were actually waiting on the beaches for the arriving American forces. This picnic atmosphere lasted for a few months, and then the situation began to deteriorate. Still smarting from a nasty political defeat, the short sighted and revenge-minded Bush administration was pushed into this situation in the last few months of their presidential term by the moaning and whining of a bunch of international entertainers. In the weeks leading up to our involvement, we were all treated to musical concerts and gatherings complaining about the possibility of starvation in that war ravaged country. Amazingly, these entertainers were able to direct United States national policy toward an ill-planned intervention with a few songs. Before long, there were U.S. troops on the ground, right in the middle of the madness. A few months later, a weak-minded and naive Clinton administration inherited this mess, and the stage was set for disaster.

As the months dragged on and the starvation continued, insurgent forces, led by the local warlord Mohammed Fariq Adiz, began to target United Nations forces in an attempt to gain control over food distribution points. This lead to a series of confrontations with U.S. forces and, inevitably, the first American casualties occurred. As a result of this deteriorating situation, Washington deployed U.S. Army Special Operations Forces into the country to conduct a series of operations intended to capture the Somali strong man and stabilize the situation. Not being a movie, this task proved to be easier said than done. It is never an easy job to hunt someone down in their own back yard. Realistically, an operation of this sort would take several months, if not a several years. This situation found the Clinton administration subject to the same impatience attitude existing in the rest of our society. As the pressure from Washington mounted, the operational tempo increased. Military commanders are very susceptible to pressure from above however much they would like to proclaim otherwise.

On the 3rd of October 1993, U.S. Special Operations forces conducted a short notice raid in downtown Mogadishu, hoping to capture Adiz and his top lieutenants. Moving rapidly in a helicopter borne assault, the U.S. forces were able to achieve an initial success. Nineteen of Adiz's top people were taken into custody, and the ground forces prepared for a rapid withdraw. Then came the downing of a Blackhawk helicopter and the situation quickly changed for the worse. Over the next few hours, our troops found themselves outnumbered and fighting for their very survival. The story is well known, and the bravery displayed by the participants in that fight has become part of American military legacy. Unfortunately, the lessons to be drawn from that encounter were lost on the general public and have come back to haunt us in the present conflict.

In 1999, years after the battle, I was watching a televised book signing conducted by Mark Bowden, the author of *Blackhawk Down.* This well-written account of the fight has come to be widely read and eventually resulted in the production of a movie by the same title. During the signing, Mr. Bowden presented a short lecture on his experiences while researching and writing the book. At the completion of his talk, he opened the floor up for questions and one question in particular caught my attention. The query was posed by an average looking, middle-aged gentleman, and it was as much the way he posed the question as the content of it that focused my attention. With a tone of puzzled outrage, he asked the author "Can you explain to the American public how something like this could have been allowed to happen?"

With that one question, this gentleman had unwittingly portrayed the outlook of the average American on war and conflict. The ignorance of reality contained in that question was mind boggling to a person of my background. I would have given anything to have been transported into that room and allowed to retort. Fortunately, Mr. Bowden was up to the task and provided the following reply, which I have paraphrased to some degree. "I'm glad that you asked that Sir, and I have spent many hours searching for the answer to that question as I wrote this book. The answer is simply this: When two groups of people shoot at each other, some of them get hit. Some are wounded and some die. It is really no more complicated than that. It is just the way it is." Mr. Bowden, no truer words have ever been spoken.

Another incident that brought this unrealistic national expectation to light occurred in the first few days of the invasion of Iraq in 2003. A small element of American soldiers was ambushed outside the southern Iraqi town of Al Nasaria and overrun. Several soldiers were killed, and a handful were captured. One of the captured soldiers was a young woman from West Virginia and her face was immediately splashed across the television news. Soon thereafter the "How could this have been allowed to happen?" questions appeared. Some journalists speculated that this small incident indicated a complete failure of the entire operation. As the casualties mounted in the days that followed, the bleating of the media heightened and they shrieked of disaster and doom. The fact that the progress of the war was not slowing and that American forces were meeting their objectives in a fairly timely manner seemed lost in the moment. In strictly military terms, the invasion of Iraq can arguably be viewed as the single most successful operation in American history. Unfortunately, there is no way that one could have known that from the media coverage of the event.

In war casualties are inevitable

"Wars begin when you will, but they do not end when you please"

Niccolo Machiavelli

Italian statesman and philosopher

The reality of both of these unfortunate situations was that they are simply the way of warfare. In any military conflict, casualties are inevitable and they should not, in and of themselves, be used to judge success or failure. I have often wondered what the veterans of the Second World War think as they watch the nightly news. The total casualties to date, all lumped together, do not add up to the amount of losses we suffered on individual days of that conflict. Even in the Vietnam War, we had suffered far more dead and wounded by the time we reached this point.

Our ability as a society to recognize and accept this simple fact is one of the things that will determine our ability to win any war. You cannot have a confrontation using modern weaponry and suffer no casualties. In fact, history shows us that weapons of the past produced the same results. The American public has a hard time understanding this because for many years the entertainment industry has suggested that wars can somehow be fought without anyone getting hurt or killed. In these fantasy conflicts, the fight is over in ninety minutes and most of the good guys are all walking upright at the end. If this scenario is not repeated in a real conflict, then much of the general public gets scared and discouraged. They think that somehow something "went wrong," and they start to seek someone to blame and reasons to run away. Our enemies know this about us and that is why they are as persistent as they are. They think that if we see enough dead Americans, we will quit and run away. They think this because over the last thirty to forty years, we have taught them that is exactly what we will do.

Our enemies misinterpret our reluctance

I am well aware that some of our hesitation when it comes to military conflict, stems from our cultural belief in the sanctity of human life. We are not a society that simply writes people off, and we are reluctant to spend lives in some foreign venture that seems to have no definitive end. That is understandable and commendable. Unfortunately, we are up against enemies who have no such scruples. They will spend as many lives as they feel necessary to achieve their goals. In their eyes, our reluctance appears as cowardice and it encourages them to attack us at every opportunity. As long as they perceive us as being afraid to get hurt, they will do their utmost to hurt us.

The reality of military service

As this fight continues, it is absolutely necessary that the average American gain a clear understanding of what military service is all about. Soldiers, sailors, airmen, marines, reserves, and national guardsmen are people who have volunteered to go into harm's way in the service of their nation. They place themselves in positions of extreme danger, and as a result, some of them will meet a horrific fate. These are the people who carry the fight to the enemy so that the rest of us do not have to. This is a matter of pride for the majority of these brave individuals. The privilege (and adventure) of performing this task is the reason that a lot of them are in uniform. They are not now, nor have they *ever* been, people who must be protected. The reality is that they are not even people who *can* be protected, not by their fellow citizens and certainly not by some windbag of a politician looking for votes. They protect us; we do not protect them: to suggest otherwise is ludicrous. To suggest such a thing is an insult, and that is exactly the way it will be taken by most of the folks in uniform. They are not "kids" and they should never be referred to as such. If there is one group of people in our society that have assumed the mantle of adulthood, it is our military. Especially those actively engaged in combat. Certainly they are more deserving of the title then are many of their peers; busy drinking and partying while pretending to get a college education on Daddy's dime. They are far more deserving than are many people in our society whose biological age places them in the adult category.

Another side of the situation is this: For every young man or woman that has become a casualty in Iraq or Afghanistan, there have been dozens lost in other ways. These unfortunate youngsters are victims of parents who either failed in their parental responsibilities or never attempted to carry them out to begin with. They overdose on drugs or alcohol; end up as teenage prostitutes; die in car wrecks or in violent gangs. They die in the thousands and will continue to do so. Many of the ones who live will spend years behind bars; some of them will spend the rest of their existence. Even if they do manage to survive and turn their lives around, they will receive none of the societal respect that comes with having served ones country in wartime. Many of the ones lucky enough to escape the more immediate dangers of modern culture end up in a worse predicament. Raised with no belief in anything greater than themselves, they live lives completely devoid of purpose or meaning. They wander through existence seeking meaning and finding none. I cannot think of a worse human fate than this. When compared with some of their peers, perhaps the ones who fall in combat are more fortunate.

Whatever the outcome of the present conflicts, one thing is true. Some segment of our society had to be woken up and given the opportunity to confront our enemies directly. This responsibility and honor fell to those in uniform. If nothing else comes out of this war, we will have among us citizens who have "been there and done that." Young American citizens who have shown courage and dedication in the face of the enemy and have gained a real appreciation for what they defend. This is the most precious asset that any society can possess. This nation needs this asset, and has needed it for decades. Now we have it.

Sadly, some of our people have died and more will die in the future. Many more will be injured, some horribly. That is just the way it is and there is nothing that can be done to change the basic nature of warfare. The only thing that can be done is to offer these brave individuals the respect that they deserve. So, shake their hand, pray for their safe return, and leave it at that. May the Good Lord bless them and their families.

Chapter 6

The Role of U.S. Law Enforcement

"Happy is the city which in time of peace, thinks of war"

Anonymous

Unlike the rest of this book, in this chapter I am going to address a specific group in our society. My words will be for them but I encourage the rest of you to listen closely. The average citizen needs this information as much as those to whom I direct it. It is not my desire to anger or insult anyone and I hope that is not the way my words are taken. It is my desire to tell the truth of our present situation and I will do so.

Of all of the American citizens involved in this conflict, I believe that it is the folks who carry guns and badges who will bear the heaviest burden. Unlike any other war that we have had, in this conflict, law enforcement is stationed on the front lines to the same degree as our military. You folks have the same responsibility to protect our society and citizens from the enemy as does our armed forces. The brutal events of 9/11 clearly demonstrated that the American homeland is part of a global battleground. Those two oceans don't mean that much any more and if the enemy has hit us here once, he will do so again. When he does, it will be a thin blue line that stands in the way. Police officers, especially uniformed patrol officers and SWAT officers, are the single group of people in our society most likely to confront a terrorist on the ground. You are our first, and in many cases, only line of defense. As a police officer you have a moral obligation to protect this society from the terrorists as well as to carry out your other duties. You may believe that you are at some sort of incredible disadvantage in this situation. You may be thinking several things. How am I supposed to be able to confront and prevail against a well-armed and fanatical enemy? Isn't any group that could pull off the terrorist operations of the last few years an undefeatable opponent? The reality is that here in the United States you are more than a match for your foe. Additionally, you have some real tactical advantages if you understand and use them.

The main advantage

In any conflict, there is an aggressor and a defender, and the defender has some inherent advantages. In this contest, you are the defending player and you own the court. You know the territory, and your opponent does not. Even if he has done an in-depth reconnaissance, he does not have the detailed knowledge of the area that you do. The ability of police officers to go from point A to point B with just a mutter from the radio has always impressed me. You know where you are going and all the ways to get there. In all likelihood, your opponents have no comparable skill level. This ability will allow you to outmaneuver your opponent during an attack. As a general rule, you and your agency have the ability to bring far more force far more quickly to the fight, than does the terrorist. This means that you will probably win the engagement. Another critical advantage that you possess is your knowledge of the law and the proper workings of our society. In other words, you know what should be there and what should not. As you drive down the street, if something is out of place, you will notice. The same sixth sense that warns you of an ongoing criminal act can warn you of a terrorist operation. The main problem that you face in this tactical situation is not whether you can defeat your terrorist adversaries, I believe that you can. I have traveled all across the United States training tactical officers, and I know that you can win a fight with a terrorist group. No, the problem is not with the individuals that make up the institutions, but instead lies with the intuitions themselves.

Law enforcement institutions and their perception of the situation

We cannot do justice to this subject without talking about lethal force. Many questions have to be answered and decisions have to be made before an incident, not after. Your department needs to discuss the issue at length and come up with some pre-incident guidance for its personnel. This is not to say that your organization should absolutely mandate when to use force and when not to do so. That decision should be left up to the individual officer, unless he or she is directed to act in some sort of coordinated effort. The central point of the discussion should focus on the willingness or unwillingness of the department to authorize lethal force in an entirely preemptive manner. Are they willing to allow an officer to kill someone, even though that individual may not have been offering a direct physical threat to the officer in question? This is the crux of the matter. What are the officers willing to do and what is the department willing to accept to protect the citizens in its jurisdiction? When it comes to the possibility of a terrorist attack, will your leadership recognize the gravity of the situation in time for you to react properly? Will the people who are in command make the right decisions in time? Will they risk their careers for the community that they serve? Do they even believe that the threat is real and are they ready to bypass normal policy and do what is necessary in the event of an impending assault? Are your commanders prepared to risk being tragically wrong when it comes to the use of force? Are they willing to roll the dice in an uncertain situation because the alternatives to inaction are unacceptable? Are they willing to do what is necessary at the time it becomes necessary? Are they willing to order a brutal application of preemptive lethal force in a situation wherein they may not have all the facts, just suspicions? Those are the questions before you.

Unlike the more typical criminal vs. police confrontations, a terrorist incident may require the officer in question to act with deadly intent in a situation where the suspect is offering no direct physical threat to the officer. In most police shootings, the threat is more or less immediate and involves the officer directly confronting the suspect. They pulled some guy over in the middle of the night and he wants to fight. That is a cut and dry situation and the officers react based on their perception of the threat. In a terrorist situation the threat may not be so obvious and, in fact, may not be directed at the officer involved. In a situation where a terrorist possesses a bomb or some other sort of deadly device, he may have to be the recipient of lethal force regardless of his activities of the moment. In this scenario the officer may have to deliver lethal force to prevent a terrorist from taking physical action that poses no actual threat to the officer. Using a radio remote control or a cell phone to activate an explosive device is a good example of these circumstances. Nobody is going to kill a cop using a cell phone but the cop may have to kill someone to prevent them from using that same instrument.

Bad as that is, I will go even further into the realm of possibilities. I can visualize a set of circumstances that may require the use of force no matter what the terrorist suspect is doing at the moment. If he or she is in control of a weapon of mass destruction, such as an atomic bomb or a weaponized disease, then they may have to be eliminated even if they are asleep at the moment of contact. In these circumstances, the potential catastrophic results of a detonation or release are unacceptable, at least in my mind. The threat has to be eliminated because if it is not, then the results will render all aspects of the threatened society null and void. This is a set of circumstances that are hard to swallow for many people in law enforcement, especially administrators. I know that my words sound extreme but if this situation happens in one of our cities, I hope that the right decision is made in time.

Are your leaders willing to risk being wrong?

In the courses that I teach, this subject has been raised many times and some lively discussions can result. Across the nation, the main concern of law enforcement seems to focus on what will happen if lethal force is used and the officers are mistaken in their evaluation of the situation. The ugly specter of post incident legal threats seems to be what everyone fears. In light of what has happened in the aftermath of many police shootings this is understandable yet, I think that the real concern is not being addressed. In these discussions, the existence of the proverbial "ACLU lawyer" and his or her vengeful action against the department is viewed as the main adversary. That possibility is always there. I would summit that the main concern should be what will happen if force is not used and the terrorists are successful. After all, what threat does a shooting review board and/or department liability present as compared to a release of a weaponized virus on the population of the city in question? How does a potential lawsuit compare with the detonation of a nuclear weapon on the downtown of a major population center? What scares you more, the possibility of being dragged into a courtroom to explain your actions or the fact that your wife and children may be exposed to a deadly chemical agent and die from it? If you fail to act in the proper moment, what will you tell yourself in the aftermath? Could you look in the mirror (assuming that you even survive the attack) and tell yourself that you did not act because you were worried about what might happen in the post incident legal arena? Will you tell yourself that you obeyed the rules and so it is not your fault that everything around you was destroyed, including the courtroom that had you so worried? On a lesser scale, think about walking through the aftermath of a suicide bomber attack on a shopping mall in your jurisdiction. Imagine looking at that horrific scene, knowing that you could have taken some action to prevent it but you had been more concerned with departmental liability. What would you say to yourself then? What words would suffice? These are hard questions to answer. Nevertheless, they must to be brought to the table and discussed realistically. All across the nation, law enforcement organizations need to face this issue and resolve to do whatever is necessary to protect the society that they serve.

You have to look for the enemy

"The quickest way to end a war is to lose it"

George Orwell

British author and journalist

The use of pre-emptive lethal force is not the only difficult subject that must be examined. Just as distressing is the question of profiling people because of ethnicity or religious affiliation. This is a subject that has caused many headaches for law enforcement over the last few decades. All across the nation police departments have had to confront this issue. As a result, there has been and official and unofficial prohibition to this approach. A situation of paralysis has been the result in many agencies. Again, that is understandable but it does not adequately address the subject. In this war against terror, paralysis is deadly.

By the rules of our society, to single out an individual strictly for reasons of ethnicity or religion is deemed to be wrong. Doing this can result in legal action against the officer found guilty of such an offense. In normal times, this approach is understandable. These are not normal times. To not look for ones enemy in a time of war is the very definition of insanity. Common sense needs to rule in this situation. If one is looking for narcotics violations, one has to look in the direction of those whose history has shown them to be routinely involved in such activities. If a given part of a jurisdiction comprises a certain ethnic group, then the search for the perpetrators of that group must be focused on that group. Nothing else is going to work. If you are looking for Islamic terrorists, then you would be advised to look at the Islamic community because the terrorists will attempt to hide among them. You could surrender to political correctness and focus your examination on the community at large but your chances of success would diminish. To put it more quaintly; if it looks like a duck, quacks a lot, poops in a pond, and has green feathers, then there is reasonable chance that it is a duck. Is it an Al Qaeda duck? Maybe it is and maybe it isn't but it is a duck. You have at least started in the right place. To look for prairie dogs, for fear of insulting the ducks and their self-righteous lawyers, will not be helpful in these circumstances.

Radical Islamic organizations tend to recruit within their own ethnic and religious communities. This only makes sense as it is difficult to convince someone to die for Allah if they have never heard of the fellow. An excellent book entitled *The Al Qaeda in Europe* backs up this theory. The author of this work makes the point that many of the radical Islamic terrorists of the last few years were recruited, not in their homelands, but in their adopted European nations. This list includes those involved in the 9/11 attacks. Feeling cut off and alone, they gravitated toward their own religious institutions and were ensnared by the radicals within that institution. Birds of a feather flock together and you will waste your time looking for Osama bin Ladens' boys at the local Rotary Club or Baptist Church. If for any reason you think that this form of terrorism threatens your jurisdiction, you had better start checking out the mosques. That is where you will find them; sequestered within a community of people of the same background.

The cultures of the Middle East and the Persian Gulf are unique and have their own peculiarities. In general, they are a people given to public displays of emotion, especially anger and hatred. Think of how many times you have turned on your television set and seen a howling mob of these folks dancing in the streets. Unlike western cultures, these people see no need to camouflage or conceal what they feel. Indeed, emotional displays are encouraged and admired. Our societal upbringing teaches us to hold in our feelings to one degree or another. In our military and law enforcement institutions this training is carried to an even higher degree. To control ones feelings, especially when provoked, is looked upon as the epitome of professionalism in our culture. Not so with the enemy, as they practice no such restraint. Given a choice between disciplined professionalism and outraged howling they will opt for the noise every time. In a face-to-face confrontation most of them cannot disguise their hatred for the United States and you. Just get them talking and they will probably do the rest. I do not know of any law or regulation that prevents an American police officer from striking up a conversation with someone because he or she is simply curious. You did not surrender your constitutional rights when you took your oath of office. You are free to talk to whomever you want, whenever you want, just like any other citizen. You can talk to people and ask questions as much as you desire. Obviously, if you're questioning results in a legal action, then you may have to answer some questions on what led you to the encounter in the first place. Nevertheless, asking simple questions is not an infraction of the rules. Such questioning may determine much about the individual.

It's about intelligence

When it comes to gathering intelligence on our enemies, the defensive structure of this nation has descended into laziness and incompetence. Unfortunately, it doesn't look like this condition will improve any time soon. At the national level, this situation is represented by a total reliance on wiretapping, monitoring of the internet and satellite imagery. This dependency on technology alone led us directly to 9/11 and it will lead us to the next debacle. At the state and local level, departments sit around waiting for e-mails from the FBI. They do this because they assume that the federal government has some magical source of information on potential terrorist activities in their jurisdiction. More than likely, the FBI doesn't have any more information than the locals and would be loath to share it in a timely manner if they did. The simple facts are that when it comes to watching the bad guys, the local agencies are pretty much on their own. Yes, they may get a heads up from the feds about a suspected attack. It is even possible that this warning may actually come in time to do something about it. Then again, *there may be no warning at all from higher levels*. They may not have the information and even if they do, they may not be set up to deliver it in time.

Another thing that you must keep in mind is that an impending attack may have developed solely in your jurisdiction and will be carried out solely in your jurisdiction. Law enforcement agencies at all levels need to develop their own intelligence gathering capabilities when it comes to terrorism. Nothing else is going to work. The terrorists are spread across a wide range of cities and can attack from any direction. American law enforcement agencies must develop the same ability to penetrate terrorist groups in their jurisdiction that has been developed to penetrate groups of drug traffickers. They have to have their own warning system. This will not be an easy task and will require continuous effort over a long period of time. On the other hand, it is not an impossible task. There is no culture or society on the planet that cannot be penetrated for information. Along with the effort of single agencies, there is a necessity for inter-agency cooperation.

The fussing and feuding has got to stop

"An injury is much sooner forgotten than an insult."

Lord Chesterfield

British statesman and author

I have been involved in law enforcement, both as a officer and trainer, for the last twelve years. This has given me quite an insight into this profession and its realities. One of the most disturbing discoveries that I made soon after entering this world is the culture of fighting and feuding that prevails all across the board. This is true at all levels: federal, state, and local. There are some exceptions but in general, no one wants to cooperate and work together. In most cases, the combative attitudes originate at the middle and higher levels of the institutions. In far too many cases, it involves nothing more substantial than ego and immaturity. It is a war between individuals that don't like each other and the amount of harm that may come about as a result of this situation is potentially catastrophic. All across the nation, law enforcement agencies fight, fuss and feud like a classroom of unruly fourth graders. They refuse to cooperate or share information and if you listen to them, you would come away with the impression that the main threat that they face is not the criminal or terrorist element but each other.

I have witnessed this set of circumstances again and again over the years. So ingrained is this feudal mindset that nothing seems to change, no matter how extreme the circumstances. Things continue unchecked year after year until the day comes that they are presented with a serial killer, a Hurricane Katrina, or a 9/11. On that day, many of them stand stunned and immobile, waiting for someone (usually the federal government) to come and bail them out of a situation to which they made the main contribution. In these circumstances, the rescuing agency is expected to arrive and solve the problem immediately and without flaw. The new arrivals are expected to pull off this miracle despite decades of laziness and in-fighting on the part of those they have come to help. They are further expected to solve the problem despite the continuance of non-cooperation during the aftermath of the event.

Try as I might, I can find no upside to this situation. There is no benefit to either the institution or those it serves. American citizens have needlessly died as a direct result of this combative law enforcement culture and they will continue to die. When there is a serial killer on the loose, this war-like attitude among responsible agencies will allow him to claim more victims than he would if they cooperated with each other. In the event of a large scale disaster like Katrina, citizens will die waiting for rescue, while the responsible agencies scuffle over who is in charge. When it comes to terrorism, this set of circumstances will lead us to the next 9/11 or much worse.

Leadership is the key

"Leadership is not about being nice. It's about being right and being strong"

Paul Keating

Australian Prime Minister

If you are a member of a law enforcement institution and these words make you angry, so be it: I stand by my statements. After a dozen years of teaching law enforcement all over the nation I can serve up more examples of this situation than you can defend. Sooner or later this war will be coming here and if this combative attitude and culture continues unchecked, it may result in us losing the fight. If you are in a position of authority in a law enforcement organization, or other first response agency, then these words were aimed directly at you. The reality is that the rank and file, given the opportunity, will generally share information and cooperate. The problems arise at the top and are cultivated at the top. Those are the people who must rectify the situation. If your department is involved in a feud with another agency then you must put an end to it. Do everything that you can, and that includes risking your status and career. Whatever the original or present cause of the situation, it is nothing compared to the horrifying reality that will exist in the aftermath of a terrorist attack. When that day comes no one is going to care who the dominant agency was or who was perceived to be in control. If the pre-existing situation of noncooperation contributed to the situation then the surviving citizens are not going to be very happy with you. On that day, my friends, the explanations and excuses are going to sound pretty lame.

If you are in a situation where there is no actual hostility only indifference put an end to that also. The ability of law enforcement agencies to work together is vital to our ability to win this war. If you are not training and working with adjoining agencies, you and they are wrong. You are creating a hole through which the enemy can crawl. Solve your jurisdictional and command issues now, instead of trying to figure it out while the bricks are falling around you. If you want inspiration to do this, just study the sad aftermath of Hurricane Katrina.

The lesson of Katrina

A massive terrorist attack on a U.S. city is a scenario that has been on the radar screen of domestic law enforcement for several years now. Long before 9/11, this horrifying possibility has been the subject of countless drills and discussions as agencies have tried to conceptualize what the event would be like and what their appropriate actions would be. Much of this activity was based on reasonable assumptions and some guesswork, a theoretical model, so to speak. Unfortunately, theory has become fact and we now have a real example in front of us. The situation in New Orleans in the aftermath of Hurricane Katrina contained every possible aspect of a weapon of mass destruction attack on an American city, save one. The situation was brought about by an act of nature instead of man and that is the only major difference that I see. It would be foolish if we did not take advantage of this opportunity to look at this event for lessons learned. To totally examine this incident will require far more space than can be contained in this book, so I will present to you the two most valuable lessons that I took from the situation.

Lesson one: Never say never

My position as a Weapons of Mass Destruction instructor for Louisiana State University has afforded me the opportunity to travel the country and interact with tactical law enforcement officers from all over the United States. One of the statements that I have continuously heard during the conduct of these courses is "We will never do this." This statement is usually made by a class participant while conducting one of the more difficult aspects of the training. The supposition behind this erroneous statement is that the agency involved will never have to perform the said tasks because they fall outside the description of their day-to-day duties. The further supposition is that there is some sort of mythical, magical, prepared agency that will automatically show up during such an event and handle the situation for them. The events that occurred in New Orleans following the levy failures clearly demonstrated the fallacy of the "We will never do this" theory. As those days passed, many police officers and their administrators found themselves doing things that they would have never imagined beforehand.

Inundated with hundreds of thousands of evacuees, police commanders in cities adjacent to New Orleans found themselves in the difficult position of deciding how to deploy their meager forces. On one hand, there was the moral obligation to help those in New Orleans and on the other hand, the necessity of containing a deteriorating situation in their own jurisdiction. These leaders soon had no choice but to work their personnel 24/7, knowing that this was a situation that could not last. At the same time those commanders had to contend with dwindling gasoline supplies: a situation that had the potential to shut their agencies down. Multiple small, part-time, SWAT teams found themselves performing military like missions that looked more like something happening in Baghdad than the United States. Tactical officers boarded military helicopters and escorted the managers of the New Orleans power grid into the thick of the looting and killing so that they could assess the damage. Agencies in the cities surrounding New Orleans had to deploy their personnel with all the necessary supplies and equipment over distances of up to 100 miles and recover them each night. Tactical officers made incursions by shallow bottom boats miles into flooded neighborhoods to rescue citizens and control the madness.

In the city of New Orleans, life for the tactical unit and uniformed personnel bordered on insanity. These few individuals found themselves cut off and alone for several days. Food ran out, water ran out, and even ammunition ran out. The conditions were made worse by the desertions of scores of their fellow officers. In all of these situations, the commanders and officers involved simply did what they had to do. There was no magical agency coming to the rescue from Washington D.C. There were simply the tasks at hand and the obligation to perform those tasks. The lesson is obvious folks: never say never. No one that I know has a crystal ball that allows a view of the future. No one that I know receives e-mails from Al Qaeda telling them what is and is not a potential target. Therefore, I would suggest that no one can tell, with any degree of reliability, what will or will not happen. I simply hope that when it does happen you do what you have to and you do it well.

Lesson two: Get ready now or you will wish that you had.

The lack of preparation on all levels for the aftermath of Katrina was stunning. I don't understand this, because while terrorist attacks usually come as a surprise, hurricanes give quite a bit of warning. The possible destruction of the city of New Orleans due to a catastrophic storm is a scenario that has been discussed (literally) for centuries. The lack of preparedness was all encompassing and again, I don't have room for the totality of it in this chapter. I will simply recount the factors that had the most effect on law enforcement and the *single prominent factor* was what I have already mentioned: the total refusal of most of the responding agencies to work together.

Who was going to be in charge seemed to be the main topic of concern. Everybody wanted to lead and nobody wanted to follow. The obvious result was that instead of having two to three hundred officers working as part of a single effort, there were multiple fifteen to twenty man units working totally alone. This problem was bad enough on the local and state level, but with the arrival of the federal response, it got much worse. The problems with this scenario are obvious and it greatly reduced the effectiveness of the overall response. We will never know if any American citizens perished as a direct result of these circumstances but the question is a valid one and I personally believe that some of them did. In a situation such as this, it is absolutely necessary for law enforcement agencies to work as one. This means deciding the issue beforehand and requiring all involved organizations to stick with that decision. The aftermath of a catastrophic attack on your city is not the time or place to debate issues of jurisdiction or control. The rank and file of most agencies, left to their own devices, would prefer to work with one another in a concerted effort. Again, everyone knows that the problems tend to arise in the command levels of the competing organizations, so that is where the solution lies.

There is also a physical side to preparations. While some of these responsibilities are obvious, others are not. Circumstances arose in the days following Katrina that were not anticipated by anyone. In fairness, I don't know if all of the events could have been anticipated, but hindsight is twenty-twenty and we should take advantage of that fact. The main logistical problem for the agencies directly in the effected area was the destruction of much of the infrastructure upon which they relied. District stations were gone; vehicles were lost; communications were lost; and the ability to travel throughout their jurisdiction was severely restricted. Food and water became a problem along with the basic human need for shelter from the elements. For the agencies that responded from the surrounding area these conditions limited their ability to remain on site for any extended length of time. Agencies that came from other states had to arrive with tons of supplies in order to be effective. Human beings can only operate for so long in these conditions and time is running out from the very beginning. The involved officers needed safe ground to come back to and they needed it quickly.

If you do not have food and water pre-positioned around your jurisdiction, you should get to work on that issue immediately. In the aftermath of a catastrophic attack, you are not going to have an effective police force if there is nothing for them to eat or drink. Sitting around thinking that the feds will come to the rescue is not the answer. They will get there eventually, but you are probably still going to have to run the show. Transportation is another issue that will raise its ugly head. If your vehicles survive the event will you be able to refuel them? If the majority of your vehicles did not survive the event where will you get replacements? Are there any pre-event agreements with other agencies for help of this kind? In New Orleans and the surrounding area, gasoline became an issue within a couple of days. It is amazing how much fuel is consumed with just day-to-day law enforcement activities. In an event like Katrina, the consumption rate increases dramatically, so you had better know where to get gas. Communications is another problem that must be considered. In this scenario, it is the weakest link and you can rely on it to fail when you need it the most. In the early hours of Katrina *every* communications system failed to one degree or another. When this happens, what is your back-up plan? The list will go on and on and these issues must be addressed beforehand if there is to be any chance of dealing with them effectively during the event.

The aftermath of Hurricane Katrina should be studied in-depth by U.S. law enforcement for years to come. The lessons are many and we don't even know the majority of them yet. As the years pass, they will come to the surface and the wise will heed them. We have been provided with a working model of the potential aftermath of a massive terrorist attack on one of our cities. We would be fools to not take advantage of it. As for me personally, the things that I witnessed during this situation have served to deepen my commitment to share these lesson with others.

As I stated at the beginning of this chapter, it is not my desire to anger or insult anyone. I am simply telling the truth as I have seen it, firsthand. When it comes to the War on Terror there are some problems with law enforcement in this country. Those problems need to be fixed to the fullest extent possible. If they are not, then we may well lose in the end. As the years pass, much of this war will be on your shoulders. I know that isn't necessarily fair but it is the lay of the land. This war is different from our previous ones and it will be fought in different ways. Police officers will have a key role in defending this nation during this war and that should always be in your mind. In this conflict there will be no room for denial or indifference. So, fix the problems that you can and train hard. Stay brave, stay strong and keep your eyes open. When the time comes to act-and it will come-act without hesitation. Much is depending on you.

Chapter 7

The Role of the Citizen

"No arsenal, or no weapon in the arsenals of the world, is so formidable as the will and moral courage of free men and women."

Ronald Reagan

40th President of the United States

We have some flaws in our society that play right into the hands of our enemies. These failings are manifested in the outlook and attitude of far too many of our citizens. All of the insane Islamic Mullahs and their flag-burning, howling mobs do not have the ability to bring about our defeat. We alone have that capability and that may be right where we are headed. We have some problems, Ladies and Gentlemen, and if we do not get a handle on them then we will lose this war faster than the Al Qaeda can win it. When you couple the apathy and ignorance of the average American with a lack of ability to place anything into its proper perspective you have a lethal combination. We would not be the first society that fell apart over these issues. Additionally, it is our desire (demand actually) to be continually entertained and our seeming lack of capacity to concentrate on anything but pointless entertainment that places us in peril. Friends, I have not lost a moments sleep over what the Al Qaeda may or may not do. I have studied these people all of my life and they do not scare me a bit. On the other hand, I have lost a lot of sleep and will continue to do so, worrying about the childlike ignorance of many of those around me and their ingrained willingness to run away from difficulty.

We cannot be a strong nation without strong citizens. We cannot show a united front to our enemies with a population that is perceived by the rest of the world to be weak and cowardly. We cannot have a country that is able to persevere during hard times if the individual citizens cannot persevere during normal times. Any clear eyed look at human history will show us that bad days far outnumber the good days and that is just the way it is. Everyone would be better served if more Americans grew up, dried up their tears and faced the realities of existence on planet Earth. When a nation and its future are threatened, much relies on the willingness of the average citizen to rise to the occasion. Rising to the occasion means many things but primarily it means understanding and accepting the reality of the situation.

Understand the threat that you face and how vulnerable you are to it.

Most Americans go about daily life taking for granted many of the things that make that life possible, such as water, food, and electricity. If they think about these things at all they most likely view them as some sort of guaranteed asset. Water is there because we need it and it is the responsibility of some faceless individual or institution to provide it. Water is something that comes because we turn on a tap. Electricity is there because we put a plug into the wall and food is something that magically appears in a grocery store. Gasoline is a commodity that we get because we drive up to a pump and while we may moan about the price we expect that it will always be there to buy. In the aftermath of a terrorist attack, these assets may no longer be available. Here is a real life example of this possibility.

Nestled deep within the industrial area surrounding a major U.S. population center is a small chemical plant that produces chlorine products. The small size of this facility (about three acres) grossly understates the critical role of the plant. Industrial strength bleach is the main product created at this location and the bulk of the material is used for water treatment in the major population centers of about four states. If this resource were to be put out of commission the result would be a loss of fresh water and sewage treatment for about thirty-five million people. How long such a situation would last is anyone's guess but it could continue for several weeks to several years. It may eventually be fixed but in the meantime the misery index for those unfortunate enough to be living in the affected area would be high and eventually lethal.

If you and your family are living in the area affected by the loss of this facility the first few hours would pass without much change. Temporary unavailability of fresh water is something that we all have had to face a few times and we just get through it. Generally this comes about as a result of damage to the water mains or the performance of maintenance on the system. When the water is shut off, everybody knows that it will come back on. The circumstances are short-lived and it is more a matter of inconvenience than anything else. Usually, the purchasing of bottled water dramatically increases and that may create a temporary shortage at your local grocery store. Once the water comes back, everything quickly returns to normal and the only effect is a small spike in the profits of the convenience stores and retail food outlets.

On the other hand, what if the water did not come back on because there was no way to bring it up to safe health standards? What if the system was destroyed by a massive explosion or contaminated by radiation and not able to be brought back on line? If the situation happened in a small location, then it would not be so bad. The few citizens affected could be supplied on a temporary basis, and again, we would have a situation of mere inconvenience. On the other hand, what if the loss was on a large scale? What if millions were affected instead of just a few? What if you and your family were among the millions? Life, as you know it, would cease to exist and the world around you would become very ugly.

The food stores would be sold out in a matter of twenty-four hours or less. Certainly they would be re-supplied, but that volume would not even begin to keep up with normal demand. Sure a lot of people drink bottled water but they rely on a main system for most of their consumption. As the hours and days passed the situation would go from bad to worse. Human beings can actually go for a considerable time without a normal intake of food. Water is a different story; our bodies would quickly succumb to dehydration. Consumption of soft drinks or an endless variety of other beverages will not and cannot take the place of water. Sooner or later the high sugar content in all of these products will induce an extreme level of thirst in the average individual. If the seasonal temperature is high, the situation will deteriorate that much faster. Within a few days you will be living in an insane asylum as the desperation level climbs. In this scenario, evacuation may not be an option as the sheer numbers of affected people make this impossible. After all where would you evacuate more than thirty million people? Any destination would overwhelm the water system at that location and add the local populace to the list of those affected. Even if, by some miracle, there was a sufficient supply of water for drinking the situation would still be wretched. Not being able to take care of basic hygiene would become a problem of similar magnitude. Sure we can all go without a bath for a few days and some folks I have met must be rehearsing for just such a situation. On the other hand, what would your life be like if you had to go without this benefit for a month or two? What would you do then? Forget the adults, what about the children? How would you clean up a messy infant? What if your baby had diarrhea and you did not have the water at hand to take care of that? How long would it be before you had a real health issue with the child?

If this scenario actually happened and the shortage of water was to be long term an even more lethal situation might develop. Before a total breakdown of society occurred, or a large amount of deaths, the federal government and the municipality affected would have to think about turning the water back on, untreated. Believe me they will seriously consider this option if the alternative is to watch thousands of people die. Now here is a dangerous situation: untreated water means diseases and not the tame ones either. Cholera, dysentery, hepatitis, and other maladies would quickly take hold in the affected population. These sicknesses would spread fast and soon overwhelm the medical establishment, resulting in death on a large scale. If you were one of the few survivors you could consider yourself lucky. The chances of your entire family coming out of such a situation unscathed are zero. All that from just shutting off the water.

Folks, I saw the plant first hand and was stunned at how critical it was and at the same time totally vulnerable. I was extensively briefed on the results of it being shut down and if anything, I have down-played the scenario. If it were to happen more than a few of the people who will read this book live in the area that would be directly affected. More than a few of them would die as a result. Think about that the next time some idiot who has forgotten how to shave (Michael Moore) comes on your television and tells that there is no terrorist threat to you or your family. Friends, there is always a terrorist threat and *you and your family* are directly in its path. If imagining this scenario frightens you, it was my intention to do exactly that. Fear is not necessarily a bad thing. Fear can be a friend as well as an enemy. It can goad people into taking critical actions that may well save their lives. A healthy dose of trepidation about the future would go a long way toward making vital changes in our national outlook.

Develop a set of realistic expectations about your society and the world around you.

We need to develop a more reasonable outlook on life. We need to realize that perfection is only rarely achieved. If we intend to demand it of others then we need to be more willing to show it ourselves. If the average citizen were required to show a fraction of competence and skill that they demand of their institutions they would fail in the first five minutes of the first requirement. Most modern Americans are physically and emotionally unequipped to deal with dangerous situations. Yet they demand that others achieve this goal no matter what the circumstances. If all their problems of the moment are not magically fixed when they see fit to demand it, they want to moan and cry. Our children tend to do the same thing but we can understand when they act up. The adults should not get off the hook so easily.

97

People who serve as part of the governmental system or critical infrastructure are people just like us. They are subject to all of the failings inherent to human beings and they will not always do the right thing. They may not do the right thing even if that were their original intent. In fact, the situation in question might not allow for any immediately workable resolutions. In the aftermath of Hurricane Katrina, I lost count of the number of people I heard who were moaning about the slow federal response to the disaster. Yet I heard none of them offer details as to exactly what the feds might have done had they been there sooner. So far no one has appeared on my television screen and realistically detailed what they might have done differently. The whiners only talk about what did not happen but never discuss how they could have made things better. Even if these arm chair coaches found solutions those solutions came with 20-20 hindsight long after the event. No one has even suggested the possibility that, in many cases, there was nothing that could have been done; which is far closer to the truth of the issue.

Realize that life is not a movie and has no obligation to turn out like one.

We have now come to the point in this country where a significant number of our citizens cannot tell the difference between fantasy and reality. When it comes to a catastrophic event many Americans only reference point comes from the imagery of a television set or movie screen. Ideas about war, natural disasters and other such occurrences are completely skewed by this perspective. As a result, when real life situations do not meet their Hollywood-generated expectations citizens tend to get angry. This exact situation came about in the aftermath of Hurricane Rita in 2005.

Rita slammed into southeastern Louisiana and the gulf coast of Texas just four short weeks after Hurricane Katrina had destroyed New Orleans. As the storm approached landfall, the State of Texas made the difficult decision to conduct an evacuation of Houston. Compared to the earlier evacuation of New Orleans, this was a much larger operation: up to four million citizens entered the interstate system to flee the area. Problems arose quickly, mostly due to the sheer numbers of people involved. Vehicles sat for hours in traffic jams and some of them broke down or ran out of gas. This resulted in even more problems with traffic jams. The same problems occurred three days later when the evacuees began to return home. Over the next few weeks, the local and national media treated the rest of the nation to story after story on how incompetent the State of Texas had been in conducting the operation. In actuality, there was nothing wrong with the Texas evacuation. For its size and scope, combined with the time available to carry out the plan, it could be considered perfection. The people who complained did so because it was not as neat and clean as something they might have seen in a movie.

When it comes to warfare, the inability of the average citizen to tell the difference between fantasy and reality gets worse. The overwhelming majority of American citizens have never been in combat and have no military experience whatsoever. What they do have is decade after decade of Hollywood's version of this event. When real war has the audacity to not look like a movie, uncertainty and confusion arise. If the conflict is not over in ninety minutes with perfect results then the average American is going to ask what went wrong. If there are casualties and bad days then many people think that all must be lost and disaster is imminent. The fact that our drama-addicted news media tend to focus solely on the bad days does nothing to help this situation.

The reality is that all wars are a mess to one degree or another and many things will go wrong as the fight progresses. This present conflict is no different. The average American needs to understand that real players in such an event must conduct activities without the benefits inherent to a Hollywood production. They have no magical window that they can peer through prior to carrying out combat operations. War is something that can only be honestly viewed in the big picture. The only valid question that can be asked is whether overall success was achieved. In fact, the definition of success can and will change as the conflict progresses. It has always amazed me to hear un-initiated civilians, who have never served a single minute in uniform, come on my television and attempt to critique an ongoing conflict. That they know less than nothing about such a venture and are unqualified to offer a serious opinion seems to be lost on them.

Realize that there are more important things in life than entertainment.

"Science may have found a cure for most evils; but it has found no remedy for the worst of them all—the apathy of human beings"

Helen Keller

Blind and deaf American author, activist and lecturer

I was recently in Kansas City teaching a course to local law enforcement. The location chosen for the final exercise was the Kansas Motor Speedway, scene of NASCAR's Winston Cup race. These are well funded and organized events and all of the racetracks must meet high standards. As I walked around the facility, the care and maintenance that went into the place was obvious. Everything was neatly painted and groomed: not a blade of grass was out of place. Because we often use such facilities in our training exercises, I have seen them all across the country: sports stadiums, racetracks, amusement parks and such. The American landscape is full of such altars to the God of entertainment. Never in human history have a people had more money and time to spend on entertainment. Never before in human history has there been a people so focused on entertainment. Never before in human history have a people been so focused on entertainment in the middle of a war for their cultural survival. This is a first and it is a dangerous first.

Entertainment, folks, is just that-entertainment. This is something that should be way down on the list of importance in regular life, much less in a time of war. The entertainment of the moment has nothing to do with the future of this nation. Walking through the public schools around the country and finding them in as good a shape as the sports facilities is something about which I can only dream. To have the same enthusiasm shown toward the education of our children that is demonstrated at sporting events would go a long way in securing their future, wouldn't it?

Realize that there is no nuclear option

I have lost count of the number of times I have heard someone say "We should just nuke them into the Stone Age." Ladies and Gentlemen, that is not going to happen and it is a typical lazy American way of thinking. Contained within such an utterance is the erroneous belief that there is some easy and quick fix to the situation. Again, a typical modern American thought process. The United States of America is not going to fire a nuclear weapon at anyone to change the current state of affairs. Not only would that be morally wrong but it would place us in a position of being castigated by the rest of the world for generations to come.

In the same vein, the solution to our problems is not necessarily to "bomb them into oblivion" or "turn them into a parking lot." There is a degree of proportionality and subtlety necessary in this conflict and the solutions may never be as cut and dried as we would like. More than likely, the day will never come when we see a clear cut victory, only a defined lessening of the threat. We are going to have to fight this thing one day at a time and some of those days will be bad ones. In the end, this war is going to come down to killing the terrorists one by one. That task will be conducted on the ground by the people who have the courage and conviction to do it and it will take generations to accomplish. That is just the way it is.

Learn about the world around you and America's place in it

"If a nation expects to be ignorant and free, in a state of civilization, it expects what never was and never will be."

Thomas Jefferson

Third President of the United States

The ignorance of the average American citizen can be astounding and, in a conflict such as this, it is dangerous. When I see Jay Leno asking simple questions to average people and witness their almost prideful ignorance I find nothing funny. When I talk to college graduates and discover that they cannot recount anything substantial about U.S. history or the contributions that we have made to the human race, I am disgusted. The fact that they can recount the silliness of the previous night's sit-com (almost verbatim) deepens my disgust. In a war for cultural survival this ignorance is potentially deadly. I cannot think of a more pathetic statement than, "I just don't understand what this is all about." Folks, if you don't understand then you need to find out. Try exchanging a so-called reality show with *The History Channel* for a few nights and you will be amazed at the things you learn. If you concentrate on the present situation and watch for shows on this subject, you can become quite knowledgeable. American history, the nature of western democracy, the origins of Islam and the recent history of the middle-east serve as examples of topics to look for. Obviously, there are far more important things to focus on these days than a sit-com or some sporting event. Make a few trips to your local library and set about filling in the gaps of your knowledge. You may be surprised at the things you discover. When you are able to recount some general history of the Middle East and the Persian Gulf, you will be making good progress. Remember this; your enemy has no such shortcomings. They understand what has happened in the past and that is the sum of their focus.

Understand that the world is not ending because it was a bad day

"The nature of bad news infects the teller"

William Shakespeare

English playwright

Modern Americans may be the most easily psychologically defeated people in the history of the human race. Many of us are ready to declare total defeat when the going gets a little rough or unpredictable. I often wonder what some of the folks of the past would think of us if they could be brought into our time. What would Lewis and Clark and the members of the Corps of Discovery think of their fellow citizens if they could hear us moan about our supposed tribulations in modern life? What would the veterans of Gettysburg or Antietem think if they were to hear all of the defeatist talk going on about the conflict in Afghanistan or Iraq? What would the folks who stood at Lexington and Concord think about our willingness to throw in the towel as soon as the situation looks a little grim? These people had to face situations that we can only imagine and they did so knowing nothing about the outcome Yet they managed to stay the course. They could not have prevailed with the attitude of the average American citizen of the twenty-first century.

Personally, I sometimes find it hard to not get discouraged when I see people around me who are ready to declare defeat at any moment. The aftermath of the Gulf Coast hurricanes serves as a good example. The destruction was wide spread, to be sure. In some areas, the destruction was total. On the other hand, much worse things have happened; some of them only recently. The effects of the tsunami in Indonesia and the Indian Ocean makes what happened to New Orleans look like the aftermath of a gentle summer thunder storm. The earthquakes in Pakistan caused death and destruction of a scale far greater than that which was suffered in our disasters. Many nations, including ours, have suffered far more military casualties in warfare than we have in this conflict and these nations still maintained the will to fight. Compared historically, modern events haven't been so bad. Yet there are those who think that the world is getting ready to spin out of orbit.

Don't be swayed by the ravings of the media

"There are laws to protect the freedom of the press's speech, but none that are worth anything to protect the people from the press"

Mark Twain

American author

A great deal of our defeatist attitude and our willingness to be continually discouraged comes from the effect of our news media. For decades they have bombarded the American citizen with a message of desperation and hopelessness. The last thing these folks seem able to do is say something good about anything that this nation has done or stands for. In fact, unless these people are celebrating some failure of our society, they seem unable to speak at all. Finding another brutal dictator to love or displaying outright cowardice in the face of radical Islam seems to cheer them up a bit. Other than that, they can be a pretty downcast bunch. If you listen to them long enough you will be hard pressed to find a reason to go on living. Just this morning I was listening to the news shows and for over half an hour the gist of the talk went like this:

"Ignorant people of America, the end of the world is now at hand and all will soon be lost. Wars rage in the Middle East and, as you all know, nothing like that has ever happened before. Israelis fighting Arabs is something that we have never seen prior to today and, therefore, World War Three must be upon us. As a result of this conflagration gasoline will soon be five hundred dollars a gallon causing a total collapse of the world economy and mass starvation will follow. Of course this may not matter because global warming will soon raise the average temperature on planet earth to over one thousand degrees and will extinguish all life in that manner. Now, it is possible that before that happens, a Gulf Coast hurricane will

slam into us and physically tear the North American Continent in half. One half will remain in place and the other will go spiraling into the Atlantic Ocean. This will unbalance the rotation of the planet and send us on a one way trip into the sun."

"In other news rouge, third world nations are launching missiles in our general direction, indicating that they don't like us. Pay no attention to the fact that they were only capable of hitting the open ocean and that their prized projectile only worked for thirty seconds before blowing up. The fact that they tried at all obviously indicates that they possess some modern arsenal and will soon turn us all into radioactive dust. Actually, the fact that they are mad at us to begin with is the important thing as this feeling on their part indicates that we are invalid as a culture and therefore have no right to survive their inevitable attack in the first place."

"Iran and other Islamic nations are now being run by insane fanatics who hate the western world. As this has never been the case before, it must certainly be a sign of the end to come. The smoldering contempt in their serial killer eyes should cause us to embark on a journey of introspective self criticism and result in our asking if perhaps we are not the real problem, and maybe it is time that we ceased to exist. Be sure that you tune in later tonight when our well selected guest panel will continue on in this vein. This show will only be interrupted occasionally by volume enhanced commercials, blasting you with suggestions that the only way you are going to find happiness in life is to buy the right toothpaste, shampoo, candy bar, insurance policy, etc. At the top of every hour you will be treated to a few moments with the vapid, hamster faced, twit of the moment, and she will make sure that you are aware of the latest horrific, currently developing scenario. If there is no horrific, currently developing scenario, then she will recount the details of the past days as if they had just happened."

Once we have covered all of the more mundane subjects, we will the dive right into the news of real importance. We will treat you to the sight of an aged, wrinkled, drug riddled celebrity, and cover in detail his or her attempt to crawl back into the national limelight.

We will listen in breathless anticipation for them to heap scorn and derision on the Bush administration and expect you to do likewise.

Obviously, I am being sarcastic here, but not by much, (besides, one of the most effective ways to demonstrate absurdity is through absurdity.) With the message that the world is ending and America is the source of all the planet's evil, the media has continuously reinforced the idea that they must stand between the average citizen and reality. Listening to them carry on, I sometimes wonder how we managed to survive as a nation and a culture before they wandered onto the scene. How did we manage to live our lives, pursue careers, raise families, or fight wars before they came along to show us dumb peasants how it was to be done? How did we get through all of those centuries without some self-righteous anchor person telling us that the desert is hot, dry, and dusty, and the ocean is cold, wet, and salty. As if somehow we could not figure those facts out for ourselves! My all-time favorite was years ago when *Time Magazine* released the stunning revelation that men and women were actually born different. Good thing for us that they chose to share *this* information. What in the world would we have done if they had decided to keep it to themselves? Another example of their condescending arrogance surfaced in the aftermath of 9/11, when the possibility of arming airline pilots had come up for discussion. The news media quickly denigrated the idea, informing us that the pilots "needed to concentrate on flying the aircraft." Man alive! What a stunning revelation that was! I wonder if the pilots thought of that? Of course, concentrating on flying an airplane is somewhat difficult when there is an Al Qaeda psychopath slaughtering your passengers, or trying to kick you out of your seat.

At no time does the media in this country cause more damage than it does in a time of military conflict. They can say whatever they want, but I am convinced that a fair number of them are actually ideologically aligned with this nation's enemies. These members of the media lose no opportunity to cast our actions in a bad light and make excuses for the opposition. Just the other morning, I turned on the news in time to hear one of the anchor girls shriek the following message. "Irrraaaaqqq!" she wailed, "has become a haven for terrorist and killers!" Eyes blazing, she went on for a few minutes in this vain, explaining that this was somehow our fault. As the outraged babble continued, I had to overcome an almost irresistible urge to crawl through the television screen and set her straight on a simple fact. "Irrraaaaqqq," my friends has been a haven for terrorists and killers for its entire existence. The entire Arab world is a haven for terrorists and killers. It is part of their history and culture, and they are proud of it.

Folks, a lifetime of this hostile bombardment will take its toll whether you realize it to or not. If you are at a loss for what to do, remember that your television set came equipped with an off button. Try shutting it down for a few weeks and getting your news from the newspaper or over the internet. These sources are not that much better when it comes to content but the peace and quiet will be therapeutic. You will find that you are just as informed and not as agitated. If you are reading this book and you are a member of this profession you may be offended by what I write. Well, if you are, that is too bad. I can assure you that many of your fellow citizens are offended by *your* activities. We have watched you folks for decades and witnessed a non-stop attempt to undermine this nation at every opportunity. What is most offensive about your actions is that while you seek to harm this nation, you unhesitatingly avail yourselves to any and all of its benefits. If you are really sympathetic to the cause of our enemies then you should consider personally joining their struggle. That's right, drag yourself out of that multi-million dollar cocoon in the heart of Manhattan and find your way to an Al Qaeda training camp in the mountains of Pakistan. You would still be an enemy but folks may be able to conjure up a little more respect for you.

Believe in our cause and stay brave

"When there is no peril in the fight, there is no glory in the triumph."

Pierre Corneille

French dramatist

Winning a war often comes down to nothing more complicated than a society believing in its cause and being willing to stay the course. History is replete with examples of those who prevailed simply because they refused to throw in the towel. If we are going to win in this conflict then we must be willing to stick it out, come what may. This is not to say that everyone has to agree with every decision that comes out of Washington. The folks who lead us are fully capable of making bad decisions and they will do so as this war continues. Criticism of our government's actions is one of our rights and if we were to remove that right then there would be little point to this fight: we would be just like the enemy. On the other hand, using the Constitution to undermine our efforts and then attempting to hide behind it is a despicable act. If you really don't like this nation and you really consider it to be evil then you should probably find some other society that might suit you better. If you are basically a loyal American citizen who just happens to disagree with our leaders' decisions, well, join the club. You and I see things the same way. The difference, my friends, is this. I might disagree with something that Washington has done and I might not think that they are going about the task in the right way. At the same time, once the decision is made by those who are granted the authority to make it, I will support them all the way.

Many times in my life, I found myself in complete disagreement with the decisions of those above me while carrying out their orders without hesitation. This is not because I am a servile person by nature. I assure you that I have no such qualities. I carried out the orders of those above me because they were the ones charged with the responsibility to accomplish the task at hand. There is a belief in this country that dissention is inherently justified; that somehow, it is the duty of our citizens to undermine those in authority, simply for the sake of doing it. In this viewpoint the citizen has a duty to rebel in the face of something they don't like or in which they cannot believe. Once that rebellion is displayed, the citizens can then retire to private pursuits smug in the knowledge that a blow has been struck for democracy. If questioned or confronted on the issue, these folks will assume the air of an outraged patriot and compare themselves to the minutemen of Lexington and Concord. Well folks, I tend to see things bit differently and I take great issue with the concept that all that is necessary to be a good citizen is to argue and dissent. One of the easiest things to do in life is to criticize the actions of those above us. I have come to learn that it is one thing to criticize and quite another to perform. Anyone can look at a person in a position of responsibility or authority and say that they are doing the wrong thing. It is quite another matter to be the one who has to decide what to do. To be the critic only is a simple task; it takes no knowledge, skill, discipline or ability. Those who only sit and complain offer nothing. Those who undermine things after the decision is made, offer even less. With loyalty comes courage and as a nation we need to display more of this quality. We need to find our guts and not be so willing to shrink away from the unpleasant and dangerous. The world is not ending because we are in a war and it will not end because of a hurricane in the Gulf of Mexico. Having a little bit of faith in the future would not hurt either. If you remember nothing else about this book, remember the main point of this chapter. You, the average citizen have the power to take us either on the road to victory or the road to defeat.

Choose your path carefully.

Chapter 8

What does the Future Hold?

"The future ain't what it used to be."

Yogi Berra

New York Yankees

Accurately predicting the future is a power not given to mortal human beings. Much as we would like to have a window into the next days, months, or years, we simply do not. The best that we can do is to look at what is going on today and try to make an accurate guess. Unforeseen occurrences, both at home and abroad, may make our supposition invalid but we can still try. In this last chapter, I will contemplate what the future holds.

A few weeks after 9/11 I was sitting at the dinner table surrounded by family. Obviously, the main topic of conversation was the recent terrorists' attacks and the aftermath. There was much speculation as to this nation's response. A close relative of mine insisted we could set things right and make the future safe from any more such occurrences. No doubt, this conversation was repeated in homes all across the nation. The emotion in her voice was genuine; she felt that our country would do whatever was necessary for as long as it was necessary to do it. Believe me, she was echoing my own desires in this matter. While the events of that September day had not caught me as much by surprise as it had her, I had similar feelings. I wanted the nation to see the reality of this attack and set about doing the things we had to do to prevent a future one. On the other hand, our lack of national resolve in previous years did not fill me with confidence. I was fairly sure that we would have a strong, initial response. The invasion of Afghanistan seemed to be a preordained event; in the days leading up to the invasion our "loyal and patriotic" news media was falling over itself to make sure that our enemies knew every military strategy, weapon, and technique that we would use in such a venture. Despite their intelligence sharing effort, I knew that we would probably see a relatively quick victory. The Taliban was an organization of mindless bullies with no real substance or staying power, and they had never faced a lethal challenge to their rule. When the U.S. military came to town, that was going to change. As it turned out, that is pretty much the way things went.

What had me concerned that night at the dinner table was not the immediacy of the Afghanistan situation, but the long range future. Not the months after 9/11 but the years after the event. What would we be like then? I knew that there was going to be an abstract nature to this fight and it was likely that our military would be going into Iraq or Iran. If we did, how much resolve and staying power would we have as the situation progressed? More importantly, what would we do when we started taking casualties? Would the inevitable losses cause us to cut and run? Years from 9/11, would we still be fighting the terrorists abroad or would we have retreated into scared isolationism, waiting for the inevitable attacks on the homeland? Only time would tell.

Time has passed and it is now 2007. Five and a half years have come and gone since the World Trade Center and Pentagon attacks. The invasion of Iraq happened and we are in the middle of a brutal insurgency. Scattered fighting continues in Afghanistan and casualties from the two conflicts have run into the thousands. Progress is being made but it looks like this situation will be with us for a while. So, where do we stand and what is in store for the future?

We have held the line (so far)

It is not often in life that your surprises are pleasant ones but I have been pleasantly surprised at some of our attitudes and actions of the recent years. We seemed to have learned some lessons from

9/11 after all and finally developed a little staying power. Certainly this doesn't apply to all of our citizens but it evidently applies to enough of them. Most Americans dislike the wars that we are in and that is certainly understandable. On the other hand, they like the idea of retreat even less and that attitude is the stuff of which eventual victories are made. We seem to be resigned to the fact that this thing will not be over tomorrow or any time soon. We also seem to have figured out that casualties are inevitable and we are just going to have to endure them for a while. Glory hallelujah! Of course there has now been a change of leadership in Congress and we will have to see what that brings. Our willingness to stay the course is largely based on the leadership that this nation has received. Say what you will about President Bush but one thing is sure. The rest of the world knows that when he says something he means it. They also know that he doesn't govern the nation based on media poll numbers. The world, and more importantly our enemies, know that Washington is not going to cut and run and neither is the American public, so far. So where does that leave them and us?

The present situation

For the radical Islamic crowd, this has not been a nice war. I know that our media would have you believe that we have barley scratched our foes but my sources suggest otherwise. Our quick victory in Afghanistan decapitated much of their command structure and scattered the rest. They lost thousands of their most dedicated fighters and have no reliable method to replace them. In one operation, we took away their main base of activity. Sure the enemy has the ability to carry out more attacks and, unfortunately, our casualties continue. On the other hand, our opponents have no ability to direct the course of Afghanistan's future.

Whatever the day-to-day picture is in Iraq, I would have to say that our invasion was one of the most brilliant strategic moves that this nation has ever made. Our toppling of the Saddam regime changed the whole equation. In this operation, we took the war away from the American homeland and put it smack in the middle of the

Arab world. I don't know if those in Washington were smart enough to figure this out or it just happened that way. Whatever the path, we made a good move. The war in Iraq is the only logical reason that we have not suffered an attack since 9/11. The enemy is quite simply bogged down. He cannot recruit people to come to the West when there is such a juicy target sitting right in his own backyard. Islamic militants know that they have only a slim chance of being successful on an operation in a western country. Conversely, they know how to get to Baghdad and how to operate there. They know that they will get a chance to shoot at the "infidels" in Iraq. The bad part of that situation is obvious: we take casualties. The good part of the situation is just as obvious-so do they.

Iraq

Our staying power in the Iraq conflict has shocked our enemies to the core. The whole game is not turning out according to the Al Qaeda playbook. Not only do we seem to be willing to stay the course, we seem to be able to defeat them handily on the ground. Report after report of interviews with captured Al Qaeda and insurgents confirm how shocked they are by the prowess of our military, especially our infantrymen. It seems that all of their previous indoctrination and training has led them to believe that the average American soldier could barely function in a real battle. According to this theory, our troops could not fight without cowering under an umbrella of artillery and close air support. This has turned out to be most definitely not true. Time and time again, our soldiers have prevailed against the enemy in small unit actions without the benefit of air-cover or artillery fire. On more than one occasion, our soldiers and marines have soundly beaten the enemy, despite being outnumbered on the ground. Some of these brave souls have participated in firefights that were just as intense as the battles of Vietnam and the Second World War. If this is something that our media seems unwilling to tell you, I'm sorry. They should but they probably never will.

The loyalty and bravery that have been shown by those in the military is phenomenal. It has been said that those who fought in the Second World War were the "last great generation." Well, I would have to take issue with that. Certainly the people of that generation earned the respect of the nation for what they did. On the other hand, those who are involved in this current conflict rate the same respect. Our soldiers and marines have performed to the same level as those who waded onto Omaha Beach. Fellow Americans, another "great generation" lives among us.

After Iraq

We will not stay in Iraq forever and nobody really knows what will happen when we eventually withdraw. I am confident, however, that leaving Iraq will partly open the door for a resurgence of terrorist activity in the western nations. Once they are not tied down in their part of the world, the Jihadists will come knocking on our door. When that happens, the real war on terror will begin. We will have some attacks on our soil, you can guarantee it. What that will do to our resolve and staying power is unknown at this time, but everyone had better prepare for it. The situation may take a few years to develop, but develop it will. Already there are indications that they are contemplating this move. Notes taken from the house of the recently slain Iraqi insurgent leader indicated that he felt that his side was making no real progress in Iraq. As a solution, he proposed the idea of taking the war to the streets of America. If he was thinking that way, you can be sure that others are too.

The political future

We have prevailed so far in this conflict because we have had some adequate leadership at the national level. Even those who do not like the president will admit that he is a man who does not waffle or abandon the path that he has set. Our enemies know this also. What will happen if we get someone in the White House who has no such characteristics is anyone's guess but it will probably not be good. Weak leadership in this war will place victory right into the hands of our enemies. The Europeans are going to learn this the hard way in the next few years and I hope that we don't have to learn it with them. We are going to need good leadership for the duration of the conflict and it remains to be seen whether or not the American voter can provide it.

We are not going to prevail in this conflict until we get a handle on some things back here. One of the primary ones is the specter of illegal immigration. This will require us to place just as much emphasis on the threat coming from the Canadian border as that coming from Mexico. If we want to keep out the wolf we are going to have to close the gate. There are some recent indicators that we are finally going to get serious about this problem. National Guard troops are being deployed to the southern border and the Canadian border also seems to be getting some attention. Let's hope it is not too little, too late.

In Closing

Believe me, folks, the War on Terror is a subject that I could discuss indefinitely. This focus has been part of my life for as long as I can remember and it will continue to be a major part of it. On the other hand, there is such a thing as too much information. If I were to continue on, I think that I would reach that point with my readers. Perhaps with some of you I already have. So, I will close out with a few parting thoughts. Friends, this thing will not end any time soon, so get used to it. On the other hand, life is still very much worth living and there are always new possibilities for the future. The Unites States of America is a great nation and we are all privileged to be part of this country. Our way of life is worth defending and it should be the one that prevails in this struggle.

All of the words in this book are my personal opinions and no others. These opinions represent the way I see this struggle and I make no apology for them. Naturally, you are free to agree or disagree with me. That freedom is one of the greatest things about life in this nation. If you do disagree with me, please have the intellectual honesty to come up with some *real* ideas that rival my own and base these ideas on *real* knowledge. If you cannot then the next logical step is to accept the ones presented in this work.

Fellow citizens, stay brave and stay strong, and we will see what the future brings.

In the meantime: God Bless America and you!

Recommended Reading

Here is a list of books that I recommend to those who wish to increase their knowledge about the current conflict. Obviously, these are not your only choices and I would encourage you to dig further.

The Haj, Leon Uris

For the un-initiated, this book is one of the best places to start. It is a work of fiction but maintains correct historical context. It is the story of a young Palestinian boy growing up in the 30's and 40's. Being fiction, some of it must be taken with a grain of salt. On the other hand, it has the clearest insight into the thought process of the Arab mind that I have ever read.

Ironfire; A novel of the Knights of Malta and the Last Battle of the Crusades, David Ball

Again, I recommend a work of historical fiction. This book is absolutely great. It is historically accurate and the made-up characters are completely plausible. It is the story of the Island of Malta and the last clash between Christianity and Islam prior to the uneasy truce that lasted a few centuries. Read this book and you will understand the original nature of the fight.

Al Qaeda in Europe; The New Battleground of International Jihad, Lorenzo Vidino and Steven Emerson

This one is recent and non-fiction. It is a well written examination of the Al Qaeda's activities in Europe over the last decade or so. It is also an insightful look into the mind of the modern terrorist organization.